Flower

Dr. St

The Seven Bodies Unveiled

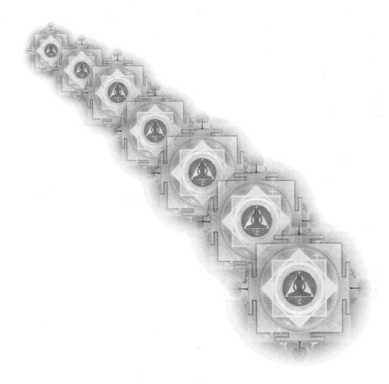

Flower A. Newhouse

Dr. Stephen Isaac

The Seven Bodies Unveiled

Bluestar
Communications®
Woodside, California

© 2001 Christward Ministry, Escondido, California

Published by:
Bluestar Communications
44 Bear Glenn
Woodside, CA 94062
Tel: 800-6-Bluestar

Edited by Evelyn Alemanni
Cover Art by Heita Copony
Cover Design: Annette Wagner
Layout: Petra Michel

First printing 2001
ISBN: 1-885394-49-7

Library of Congress Cataloging-in-Publication Data
Newhouse, Flower Arlene Sechler, 1909-1994
    The seven bodies unveiled / Flower A. Newhouse, Stephen Isaac.
    p. cm.
    ISBN 1-885394-49-7
    1. Bodies of man (Occultism) 2. Christward Ministry. I. Isaac, Stephen, 1925-
    II. Title.

BP605.C5 N455 2001
299'.93--dc21   00-064225

Printed in USA

Acknowledgments

A book of this nature is the product of the efforts of a number of individuals who contributed to its research, word processing, editing, book design, and layout. I wish particularly to express my appreciation for the generous contributions of time and expertise of Gwen Hulbert, Evelyn Alemanni, and my wife, Phyllis.

Stephen Isaac, Ph.D
Questhaven Retreat

Contents

Foreword

We who live in mortal bodies are prone to accept them as our identity, reflecting who and what we are, as if this single body must answer for not only our physical condition, but our emotions, mind, and spirit, as well. Indeed, we observe individuals who, at one time or another, are entirely caught up in one of these several states of being. This raises the question: Is the physical body with all of its various systems a totality in itself, or are we far more complex beings? After all, we inevitably come to the simple fact of death and the great question, what survives it? Those of us who are not materialists, look to what we call our souls to see beyond the grave. Yet there is evidence that more than the soul is involved. In 1902, the gifted clairvoyant, C. W. Leadbeater, published a volume entitled *Man Visible and Invisible*. In observing the human aura, he noted a co-mingling of seven bodies, each enfolding the other in ascending mantles of light.

Little has been written on this subject since the appearance of Leadbeater's classic work a century earlier. It was therefore fortunate that Dr. Peter Michel, residing in the Munich area of Germany, was familiar with another gifted clairvoyant living in California whose writings and lectures on this subject were equally illuminating. He had published most of her books in the German language and wanted to see a book of her teachings on this vital subject. Her name was Flower A. Newhouse, one of this century's most active and authentic mystics. Her principal mission was twofold: first, to re-ignite the flames of Christian mysticism; and second, to reawaken within people an awareness of the angel kingdom. For some 85 years, between her birth in 1909 in Allentown, Pennsylvania and her return to God's kingdom (at her home at Questhaven Retreat, near San Diego, in 1994) she tirelessly pursued these two missions as her life's work. Clairvoyant from early childhood, she beheld and communed with Angels and nature beings as naturally as the rest of us behold and commune with each other. Equally remarkable, when she turned her attention on the human aura, as with Leadbeater, she observed the sevenfold nature that comprises each human being. She soon became adept at reading the various conditions of the aura, detecting regions needing healing or strengthening, along with those revealing the noteworthy qualities and accomplishments of a particular person. Flower taught that the aura of each individual contains not only seven bodies but a summary of one's attributes, one's karma, and one's unfinished business. She noted that Angels working with individuals can grasp a detailed portrait of their human charge at a glance, so revealing and rich in information is the aura.

For Flower as a teacher, the human aura was her key to understanding and assisting those who became her pupils. The ability to perceive auras made it possible for her to recognize the maturity and strength of an older soul, or to cut through the defenses and blind spots of beginning aspirants, setting them on course, and seeing them involved in sincere progress. It is also these seven levels of our existence that form the bridge joining our matter-of-fact notion of the world we live in with the light-filled, mystical realm of our Creator.

Flower's work continues at Questhaven Retreat today. As one who revelled in nature, she founded her center in a 640 acre wilderness preserve some 30 miles north of the city of San Diego, California. Here, amidst the rich mantle of Pacific coast chaparral and canyons lined with native California live oaks, she and her husband Lawrence founded the Retreat in 1940 and pioneered its early years without electricity or telephones. Today, it contains the Church of the Holy Quest, Friendship House, Questhaven Academy and Library, office, and a variety of guest facilities.

It is our hope at the Retreat that readers who find this message inviting will find their way to its grounds, its many resources and pathways of enlightenment, for the journey it begins is life-changing.

Stephen Isaac
Questhaven Retreat

About the Author

Flower A. Newhouse

From the time she was a child of six, Flower Newhouse beheld Angels and nature beings as freely as most people look upon each other. Because her gift of seeing into the Inner Worlds was not understood by most adults she encountered, she soon gained the wisdom to discern and address those who would appreciate her gift of clairvoyance.

As the years passed, she was invited to speak at numerous churches and truth centers around the nation, where people valued her teachings. In 1937, when she was still in her twenties, she published her experiences with Angels in a book called *Natives of Eternity*, establishing herself as a pioneer in this field of study.

She and her husband, Lawrence, went on to found their own center and life work at a place called Questhaven Retreat in Northern San Diego County, California. Here in a wilderness preserve encompassing 640 acres of chaparral-covered hills and live oak canyons, graced by cool Pacific winds, she continued her lectures, writing, and retreats on this enchanting subject. Her fondness for these selfless, steadfast beings never faltered. Indeed, she gathered around her a number of talented artists whom she inspired over the years to capture glimpses of angelic presences. She also celebrated annually a major three-day retreat honoring the Angels on the occasion of Michaelmas at the end of September.

Questhaven Retreat, with its Church of the Holy Quest, Friendship House, Academy and Library, and a variety of guest accommodations is a unique and consecrated center to the Lord Christ. Interested readers may contact this nature sanctuary at:

Questhaven Retreat
20560 Questhaven Road
Escondido, CA. 92029
phone: 760-744-1500
web site: www.questhaven.org

The Seven Bodies

Chapter 1
The Physical Body

There is within each human being a divine destiny that began with God in the form of a spark from His Indwelling Spirit. It is the resulting God-flame known as the monad that contains the destiny of each soul who incarnates on earth. That destiny is to evolve through a succession of incarnations until, perfected now ourselves, we return once again to our origin, the Indwelling God Spirit. To accomplish this timeless journey, the spirit creates for each individual a sevenfold series of bodies arranged in ascending order: physical, etheric, astral, mental, soul, adonai, and monad. Seven, it turns out, is a sacred number by the fact that it often becomes the number of dividing points or entities forming a particular sacred concept. Sunlight passing through a prism divides into seven colors. There are seven dimensions to the inner worlds, and seven rays to the wheel of incarnation.

These seven levels of our being are the projection of the spirit of God Indwelling which permeates and infuses each of these levels (also called bodies or vehicles). They are all equally necessary to the spirit's purpose, but it is the spirit alone that is immortal, in command, and forever perfect in God. One of the principal aims of the experience of enlightenment is to awaken the individual to the needs and different expressions of the spirit's mind, emotions, energies, and physical manifestations.

We begin with the physical body, recognizing that what matters is its sound and healthful functioning. It is axiomatic in the esoteric approach to health and physical well-being to work from within, outward; and from the top, down. Indeed, if we proceed otherwise we will encounter mistakes that will require a considerable amount of time to correct. Where the physical body is concerned, there are no shortcuts. When our bodies remind us of this fact, and we are overtaken by a health problem, it is necessary to go back to square one and begin again. Only this time, we must be prepared to do it through prayer work and attitude transformation, based on the healing propensities of the Lord God Indwelling.

In projecting into existence its several bodies, the God Spirit willingly imposes limits on its own return to wholeness in order to taste or savor what each of these vestments offers in the way of experience. It looks upon these bodies as faculties that enrich the understanding and wisdom that life offers. In our turn, we will be wise to appreciate the Spirit that brought us into being for affording us all of the opportunities that the great adventure of incarnation makes possible.

Individuals who are unduly body-minded and organ-pre-occupied, perhaps because they overvalue physical appearance, including body building, clothing and makeup, put too much stress on the ease and comfort of physical life. But when we take heed of spiritual instruction, what counts is our progress as pilgrims in the journey back to our homeland in eternity: ease and comfort no longer matter. We realize we incarnate to gather experiences which become constructive as we respond constructively. Given this insight we realize the balance that this recognition brings to our exercise of choice. We learn to see all of our many faculties as deserving of our attention, one being no better or more important than another. The one exception to this rule is the glorious God Spirit Indwelling which becomes the whole exceeding all of its parts.

However, even if we are not seeking ease and comfort, or the physical satisfaction of the earth's most sensual and pleasurable pursuits, we have a physical body with which to deal. This vehicle functions under completely different laws and regulations than exist for the emotions, mind, soul, or adonai.

As we advance, we learn the laws of each dimension and how to make corrections and bring ourselves into compliance. We do this knowing that the only one who can unify the several bodies and their faculties, as well as heal them and transform them, is the ever-present God Indwelling.

To gain healthy bodies, certain necessary principles or elements must be observed. As we strive for good health we must guard against making that quest our all-consuming priority, for physical wellness is only one aspect of wholeness. Moreover, it isn't by any means the greater part. Such one-sidedness is analogous to recognizing only one color in the spectrum of visible light.

Of the several elements that benefit our health, sunshine and fresh air are the two most important natural ingredients, followed by pure water, nourishing food, personal hygiene, proper exercise, sufficient rest and wholesome recreation. This last item, like the seasoning in what we eat, adds surprise, expectancy, enjoyment and uplift to our days.

It is most important and at the same time difficult, when we are earnest in our spiritual endeavors, that we don't stress one particular element above all the others that constitute good health. It is easy to become faddish about the foods we eat, the vitamins or minerals we consume, or the exercises we adopt. The rule of the spiritual life is *balance* and it is only when all the bodies are well aligned and integrated that we have a unity of glorious cooperation and blending throughout the total selfhood. And the dynamics of this balance aren't necessarily those of equality but often may be a weighted proportion. In the attainment of good health, for example, psychological attitude is much more important than a focus on diet. This is so because we are engaging our mental faculties to guide and transform our physical bodies

— a process that accelerates with visualization and self-discipline. As we advance and grow into wisdom, we intuitively recognize what is needed to bring our physical bodies and their care into an appropriate balance.

Meditation is of particular importance in ensuring physical health. When we meditate on the physical body and our attitude is one of sincere support and positive engagement, in that moment the physical body and consciousness are one. There are no reservations or lapses of attention. It is as if a switch was thrown and a surge of sustaining energy is now moving from our consciousness into our physical being. All the while we envision this event and the brighter our vision, the more recognizable will be the feedback from the whole of our anatomy. We should feel it signaling back its response. It may come as a sudden warmth throughout our physical body or perhaps a tingling sensation emanating from our heart and passing down our arms and out through our fingertips. Particularly memorable are those occasions, often in the midst of sleep, when our entire spinal cord pulsates in rapid rhythm sending its waves of renewal throughout our entire being, leaving us refreshed and transformed. Or it may manifest simply as a peaceful assurance that all is well within.

Still, of all of our vehicles, the physical body is the most limited and in need of enlightened vigilance and insightful care—care that takes nothing for granted and avoids any one-sidedness. Our physical body is our temple of God Indwelling and, if we are caring stewards, we will keep that temple in good order. There is an additional benefit. In our daily experiences with our physical bodies we learn what is helpful and what is not. Opportunities then arise to share this knowledge with those whose lives connect with ours, often through an act of divine synchronicity. As a result, we might then offer suggestions on how to keep the body refreshed and refueled, how to cope with stress, or how to recover from weariness and exhaustion. It is this kind of giving to others that provides openings linking our lives together. It is this kind of love that our Lord Emmanuel exemplified and left as a legacy for future generations to follow.

Chapter 2
The Etheric Body

Next to the physical body, visible to one who is clairvoyant, lies the etheric vehicle, an exact duplicate fitting it like a glove. The etheric body appears to have a depth of between a quarter inch and half an inch and it gives off an auric radiance extending another three to eight inches in a healthy individual. Its principal function is to provide energy to fuel the activity every person needs simply to be alive. The connection that binds these two vehicles together is so complete that they often are looked upon as a single unit. As a matter of fact, in prayer work they can be treated as one inasmuch as what gives the physical form its quality of life is the etheric body's constant infusion of energy. It both penetrates and permeates the physical body altogether. If one is healthy, the etheric body varies in color from a silver-white sheen to a vibrant rose. If one's health is subnormal or one is in an unhealthy environment, shades of grey appear; and if the health condition is severe, darker areas become noticeable, such as blotches of a muddy brown to black.

What distinguishes the physical body from the other six vehicles are its glands and vital organs. In their place, the etheric body contains seven major life force centers, or *chakras* (from the Sanskrit term for wheels). These remarkable chakras receive their supply of energy from three sources: the Divine God-Self Within called the monad, which is fed by the everlasting God Spirit; the kundalini fire from the Planetary Logos; and the spiritual and physical sun, in a united radiation called *prana* — the Sanskrit word meaning "to breathe". Indeed, breathing and its connection with the lungs and their revitalization of our blood supply is the principal means of replenishing our reservoirs of energy.

The well-being of the chakras, which depends on adequate drafts of prana, needs to be a high priority for every enlightened wayfarer through life. The key here is a balanced approach that avoids extremes in our endeavor to keep healthy and fit.

Physical exercise, for instance, is important for good conditioning, and up to a point it increases our energy intake. But with excessive exertion the physical body becomes strained. Instead of building up our reserves of energy, the energy itself acts like a liquid which now begins to leak through the etheric sheath by way of lesion-like openings caused by the strain. Likewise, strong emotions aroused in the astral body stimulate the etheric vehicle; and should these become excessive or destructive, the normal rhythm of the etheric chakras is impeded. The result is a loss of energy that can lead to illness unless corrected. Intense negative thoughts brought on by fear or anger particularly disrupt the chakras, impairing their function and causing a drain of one's vital resources. It is not uncommon, if these go unconquered, that the physical and mental health of the individual are at risk; even death or insanity are possible consequences.

One of the first lessons an individual is taught in basic spiritual training is to develop constructive thoughts, emotions, and values. Such precepts as the Ten Commandments and the Sermon on the Mount, along with all the teachings and adages of the world's many religions, are based on the cultivation of wholesome and constructive habits of thought and conduct — what today we often refer to as positive thinking. States of mind or emotion that disrupt or depress the energy flow in our chakras are a major priority to conquer and bring to balance.

The etheric body receives its flow of energy through the chakras, entering our physical bodies by way of our nervous systems. In the form of prana it courses along the neural pathways of the body, enabling this complex system not only to be the carrier of all external stimuli but also to be the motor force that activates our muscles and other response mechanisms.

It may come as a surprise to realize a remarkable debt we owe nature devas, those beings who serve nature so devotedly. When our physical bodies were being created, these beings contributed to the formation of the human nervous system. Any impairment to this aspect of our anatomy is of concern to them. Thus, nature is an ideal setting for anyone suffering from disorders of the nervous system.

When you are low on energy and in need of renewal for whatever reason, it is helpful to go out in nature and find a large tree and put your back against it. The prana that energizes the tree will slowly enter your own etheric vehicle and bring you back to balance. It may take anywhere from ten to twenty minutes but you will notice a difference. This extends to us once again the opportunity to appreciate the work of the nature devas in fashioning our own neural architecture.

Likewise, a large rock that has been warmed in the sun will slowly release this same energy when we rest against its radiant surface. After a few minutes we will rise up relaxed and restored in a wonderful way.

Another source of prana is flowing water. When out in nature, try standing beneath a gentle waterfall, remembering that it was the sun's warmth that first drew water heavenward from the sea. In the waterfall's ever fresh downpour, energy is released; it has a sparkling quality and an aliveness that quickens our own readiness for restoration and purposeful action. This extends even to our personal well-being and body care; showers are not only more hygienic but they have a greater beneficial effect upon us than tub baths. In tubs, the streams of magnetism rapidly lose their potency once we are simply immersed in the water.

One of the most refreshing and revitalizing ways to benefit the etheric vehicle is to take up gardening. Here, as we busy ourselves with planting, trimming, weeding and the like, we are also in the presence of the very kind of devas that were originally involved in the creation of our physical forms. The green of the trees and other growing things discharge their own etheric currents. What is most beneficial, whether in a garden or a great forest, is to fix your gaze upon the leaves of trees. Most persons fail to appreciate the fact that the leaves of a tree are far more valuable than its flowers. While the flowers are vital to the reproduction of the tree, it is the leaves that produce the chlorophyll and give back to the earth not only oxygen but immense quantities of pranic energy. The simple act of looking at the green, which is the dominant color in nature, is renewing to the etheric body.

An exercise that is particularly revitalizing is to seek out a pine forest on a clear, sunlit day, lie down beneath one of its larger specimens and study the pine needles near the top of the tree framed against the blue sky. As you do, you will come to notice a flow of energy that is almost subliminal, streaming from the uppermost pine needles. You are looking upon the release of prana that is every tree's gift to life.

Prana itself has two components: vitality and magnetism. Up to this point we have addressed its expression of vitality. Its other side, however, is no less important. We encounter it when dealing with talismans — objects that have been magnetized usually by association with or the blessing of a dedicated soul. Wedding rings blessed during a marriage ceremony take on the magnetic charge given them by the officiant. Travellers often wear a St. Christopher medallion blessed for their safety. The holy water used in a christening or baptism receives the magnetic charging intoned by the presiding minister or priest. The possessions of a consecrated individual take on the magnetism surrounding that soul such that their jewelry and clothes retain this form of electromagnetic radiance.

More remarkable still, specific places come into the same manner of charging. Tombs of great souls, for example, will hold this powerful remembrance of their earthly presence. A most extraordinary instance of this phenomenon is Assisi, Italy, the home and burial place of St. Francis. The entire city is enveloped in the aura of this dedicated saint, an outshining of the spiritual magnetism his life generated. It shines as brightly today as it did at the end of his lifetime nearly eight centuries earlier. The Shrine of Lourdes, France, the site of so many miraculous healings associated with St. Bernadette, is another mantled location. As a matter of fact, every place that is sincerely consecrated to God will take on this magnetic field of energy during the period of such devotion. It is those cases of permanent mantling that are places of wonder. Besides sacred centers associated with great souls, nature itself possesses citadels and wellsprings of power that have brought their visitors to their knees in beholding such grandeur or experiencing such power. The Native Americans, in particular, worshiped their Creator in such settings.

We now turn to the relationship between the etheric body and healing, which is an especially vital and practical consideration. The state of one's health is mirrored in the appearance of the etheric body and its auric condition. Earlier it was noted that a healthy etheric aura will vary in color between a silver-white sheen and a vibrant rose. Signs of trouble with one's health appear when shades of grey invade the aura, and the darker the grey, the more serious will be the diagnosis. Because the etheric body is the exact duplicate of its physical host, the extent of the grey and the location of the darkest areas are clues as to what area in the physical body is in trouble. When the body is simply run-down, the greyness in the aura will be general with no one region in crisis. When, however, we are dealing with cancer or a serious heart condition, the locus of the more specific affliction will display a much darker and more concentrated region for investigation, often appearing dark brown or black.

A healer can recharge an etheric body that is sub par. For this to be effective, the healer needs to be a very vital individual, with energy to spare. Otherwise, if the healer lacks this abundance of vitality, it could result in a further drain of the patient's already diminished reserves. What is most beneficial is a laying on of hands in those areas that need activation. This usually involves the head with its central connection to all parts of the body via the nervous system, followed by the more specific regions of application. This simple increase of energy is often sufficient to bring about healings.

Because magnetic healers usually possess tremendous energy, they are the ones who can best massage or manipulate the body of one who suffers. Certainly it would not be wise to have someone who is passive and lacking in a vibrant vitality to touch your body, since the flow of energy could well reverse itself and go from patient to the so-called healer. On the other hand, a person with strong reserves of energy simply by being present in a room can activate those same reserves in others — especially those who are depleted. The archetypal occurrence of this form of healing was the Lord Christ. Just His presence was sufficient many times to precipitate a miracle of physical transformation among His followers. Along this line, it is important to know that for persons who suffer from an illness or severe exhaustion, their chakras will automatically turn in the direction of anyone who is strong in vitality. Moreover, the energy reserves of such a vital individual are not in danger of being depleted, for it is the nature of such exchanges that they are also resupplied automatically.

A common healing problem in our modern day world is the migraine headache. It is frequently the result of congestion in the etheric body brought on by the many demands of today's complex society. The result is a buildup of conflicting messages in the nervous system. These must be resolved and brought to peace. In treating such headaches the healer should concentrate upon the prana being sent through the head region in stronger degrees of perception. In other words, one must visualize the pranic forces doing their work, bringing order out of chaos, and freeing the head region of its congestion. The healer should stay in a prayerful mood knowing that this prana is being sent until he or she intuitively knows that enough has been received.

For all instances of healing, whether of the nervous system, the heart, the stomach or any of the other organs or structures, the light of God and the light of His prana should be focused on that particular region where the problem lies. We should see it as a fountain of light placed above the person so that the entire etheric body will be constantly rinsed free of obstructions and renewed by the pranic forces composing this inner stream of vitality.

There is much we can do to bring our lives into harmony and to a fullness of energy. When we are tense it is because we have allowed our etheric bodies to become congested. To one who has inner sight, the darkness within the etheric aura acts as a map locating where the tension lies. We must do all in our power both spiritually and physically to increase our vitality, including taking time to call it forth from God the Whole. We should appreciate it once it flows again and when we become strong enough we should remember others through prayer who are in need of greater energy. The best time for anyone serving in a healing way is when we are functioning at our finest and strongest level.

Let us also recall that the best source of prana, outside of our own invocations through the God Spirit Within and the Solar Logos, lies in our embrace of trees. The more we are surrounded by trees, the stronger is the flow of prana through our etheric vehicles into our physical bodies.

Chapter 3
The Astral Body

The astral body, more familiarly known to us as the emotional body, is at once the most challenging and most enjoyable of our seven vehicles. Emotions, after all, run a wide range of responses, both positive and negative. More than any of the other six bodies, the emotional body reveals what for the moment is going on inside of us — in particular, how we feel about ourselves, our circumstances, other people, and things in general. To the spiritual seeker it is this body that will pose the most problems, for it is through the emotions that we express feelings, ranging from anger, depression, fear, or jealousy, on the one hand, to happiness, compassion, courage, or caring, on the other.

Emotions tend to be exciting and dramatic and often we turn to them in the same manner that we seek entertainment: they make life more colorful and interesting, offering relief from boredom. But their most formidable challenge comes from what is called the lower nature — the human shadow which instinctively resists surrender and conquest. All of our petty grievances, frustrations, rebellions, and curiously our indifference and neglect where God is concerned, have their origin in our susceptibility to emotional roadblocks. There is no clearer evidence for this manifestation than our response to spiritual vows taken in earnest. They bring us face to face with our shadows — defeating our good intentions time and time again.

Just as the shadow is armed with its array of emotional weapons, the soul offers its own countermeasures. One example is Paul's recognition of *"the peace of God that passeth all understanding."* Beyond that are the two commandments given to us by the Lord Christ: *"To love the Lord thy God with all thy heart, and all thy soul, and all thy mind"* and *"to love thy neighbor as thyself."*

34

Having made the case for the importance of the emotions on the path that takes us Godward, it is time now to describe the astral body where these emotional attributes play out their various roles.

Even as the etheric body is an extension of the physical body, so the astral body is a further extension of the human form. The aura itself has an oval shape; while it resembles its physical counterpart, the astral body possesses a difference such that, compared to one's physical appearance, it may be more or less lovely according to one's state of consciousness at the moment. This can be temporary, as with a passing mood, or more or less permanent, taking on a personality trait. There are persons whose physical bodies are disfigured due to a disease or crippling condition but whose astral bodies are absolutely beautiful, because they bear their burden nobly. At the same time, others may have handsome or glamorous physical bodies but their emotional vehicles are a moral disaster. Their astral bodies will be quite disfigured and inferior.

There is one consolation for those who have struggled with their astral bodies and feel they have failed more often than succeeded. In each incarnation, we enter life with new physical, etheric, astral, and mental bodies. Only the three higher body forms — the soul, adonai, and monad — are relatively permanent. Thus, for one who has made mistakes, as have we all, there is opportunity for a fresh beginning. As we evolve, we expect more of ourselves, and so it is that each life experience allows us to upgrade our attitudes and conduct, bringing both closer to our ideal.

Complicating what a clairvoyant sees when studying a given individual is the fact that all of the several bodies interpenetrate each other, so that it is often difficult to note where one ends and another begins. A good illustration of this complication would be thinking a particular thought which arouses an emotional response, blending the auras of the mental and astral bodies. Were this a fundamental source of confusion (mixing the astral body with one of its neighboring vehicles) a wise clairvoyant might, through astral projection, visit this individual on the astral plane. Under these conditions only the astral body of the one seeking help would be visible, allowing the clairvoyant to examine it free of any interference from another vehicle.

Normally, the human aura is a summation of the energy fields of the seven bodies. The astral body can be observed as lying between the etheric and mental vehicles and tends to dominate the entire aura because of the expansiveness of its feeling nature. In the typical individual it extends between three to six inches beyond the underlying etheric sheath. In an awakened soul, this could be as much as ten or twelve inches. The astral rim of energy is so revealing of a person's place on the path that in the case of a Master — one who has perfected all of his or her human attributes — the extension would be about a mile in every direction, so luminous are the attainments of such a soul.

Turning now to ourselves, let us consider our own astral bodies. Taking humanity as a whole, few people even realize that their emotions constitute a living, dynamic body that, much like their physical form, needs its own share of care, attention, and cultivation. It, too, needs daily cleansing and purposeful exercise if it is to mature and radiate health and beauty. The average person is so absorbed in the demands of physical reality that the refining of the emotions is neglected. Yet, of all the bodies, the astral is the most difficult and demanding. The mind is much more responsive and the etheric body is even more so. The astral body, on the other hand, over-reacts to life, which is quite a different matter. It thrives on the dramatic, exaggerating its reactions all to the end of making an impact, winning attention, and controlling others.

For the person who has awakened to the quest for God, the astral body becomes a proving ground — an arena where that individual at last must take charge and begin a process of transformation that will bring this body to peace, balance, and control. Since it is our astral body that most likely will test us, forewarned is forearmed. If the aspirant has yet to live in a consciousness of faith, any change in life, along with new opportunities, is apt to arouse fear, a circumstance that greatly strains the astral body which may so easily respond with pessimism and worry.

In place of calamity, one needs to envision a constructive outcome. Every negative thought, every impulse of fear should now be cancelled and in its place shall be substituted a conscious beholding of life as it was meant to be. What actually must come into being is a training relationship between the person as a disciple and that one's astral body. Every day, every conscious moment, this emotional vehicle needs to come under surveillance, as we work on curbing its tendencies toward extremes, neutralizing its negativity, and encouraging its optimism and joy. Faced with its appetite for excitement and drama, it's well to speak to it as one would address an errant child, "That's enough, behave yourself!" Or, in the words of our Lord, "Peace, be still!" As to our attitude towards testings, it must always be constructive and appreciative. Tests form the lessons to be learned in the school of life. They constitute our next step of growth. They are, more than our times of ease and enjoyment, what counts for progress; we should never complain or resist these encounters, for they are true opportunities.

The astral body loves to be loved, so it needs to be looked upon with genuine appreciation. It enjoys pleasing us, but at the same time it can darken our day with anger, depression, anxiety, and other poisonous emotions. What the unmastered astral body craves is stimulation and the expression of strong feelings for their own sake. To the awakening soul this is a form of anarchy that must be brought to order. Confronted with a test which exposes a shortcoming or character flaw, we have an emotional reaction. Our feelings are hurt: we may choose to react defensively, rejecting the charge or perhaps become crestfallen and sink into a pit of depression. Alternatively, we can swallow our pride and respond constructively, grateful that we see what needs to be done. If resistance and denial prevail, we create an astral storm cloud that is forbidding to observe and we are left with all of its consequences as well as having taken no action to correct the fault. It is much the same if we give in to depression which leaves us unchanged and helpless. It is rising to the occasion and recognizing the time has come to take our next step of growth, that makes all the difference.

There is a human tendency to be puzzled by the onset of severe testings, as if we didn't deserve such encounters or the awkwardness of their timing. The truth is, all tests rightly come to us quite as they happen. Any given lesson would only come to us because the timing and circumstances were appropriate. In the eyes of the Higher Ones, what matters now is our response. There is only one thing to do — meet this testing situation willingly. Don't resist; don't procrastinate; don't rationalize away your responsibility. And to the person calling this to your attention, say something like this:

"Yes, you are right to point this out. I have been slow to recognize it. Thank you for your frankness and sincerity. You have my word that I'm going to see that this is corrected."

What is transforming about this response is its openness to constructive criticism and its commitment to change. It also puts one's astral body on notice that the game of life is now being played under new rules. No longer do one's emotions have the upper hand. From now on what counts is movement towards the goal of self-discipline. The old reactions of dominance or defensiveness are replaced with an emerging maturity and crafting of character. At its heart is the willingness to begin living the life and following the way which makes the astral body and its unruliness the principal target of opportunity.

The quality of responding willingly and insightfully to correction is one of the most valuable assets a soul can possess. The person who lacks this quality is significantly handicapped for he or she will be missing the liberating, illuminating and joyful ascent of the Mountain of God that is the aim of evolution and life.

Often the testing condition is physical, for example, when we are plagued by a debilitating illness. If this were your own trial, it might be difficult for you to keep your face relaxed and free of tension so as not to call attention to your illness in making contacts with others. It is nevertheless important to come to peace as best you can, for the part of you that is most likely to bear the brunt of that illness is your astral body. You have this condition for karmic reasons, therefore every way you can rise above any expression of the burden it poses cancels the karmic indebtedness underlying it more quickly. It is especially important not to be intimidated by your illness, or to retreat into martyrdom. Talk to your lower bodies, especially the physical, etheric, and astral, and announce that you are inviting God light to invade each of these bodies given in the care of the Lord Christ who has the power once more to make you whole. Then hold fast to that state of consciousness. Let nothing disconnect you, not even pain itself, from the awareness that God is moving within you to bring about healing. Hang on to that vision of your well-being faithfully and you will know the magic of God's healing power in greater comfort and a swifter return to wholeness.

The astral body, aside from its many shortcomings, is quite revealing of our motives and our truthfulness. If the personality self indulges in pretense, the aura will display the deceit by reflecting the truth. Should we pretend to like someone or something, when quite the opposite was the case, the discrepancy would be quickly registered as a grey shading in its energy band. That is how our Guardian Angel keeps track of our progress (or its absence) for she sees both the outer and inner aspects of our being.

The astral body is not always our tester. When we aspire to a higher state of consciousness, as in a deep meditation, we often sense drafts of spirit flowing through us and lifting our thoughts and feelings into realms of glory. What we feel in part is the uplift of our astral vehicles, which are now synchronized with our transformed consciousness. In a similar manner, whenever we suffer from depression, resentment, or anxiety, and we go to work on the particular emotion that troubles us, the fog of that negative condition sooner or later lifts, to the benefit of our entire astral nature. As we learn to invite God's light into our lives, it is this peaceful presence calming our restless hypersensitive emotions that is most profoundly appreciated.

Just as the astral body can be most disruptive, it also can be the source of joy and wonder, and it is these qualities that need to be recognized and nurtured. Again, talk to this part of yourself as you would to a growing child. Correct what requires correction and encourage what will benefit from encouragement. Invite this body to share in the great adventure of the journey back to God. Help it to value stillness, receptivity to the Divine, and acceptance of the new, for in those attributes lies its promise of transformation.

The astral body is harmed by overstimulation and excitement of the kind that shuts down its contact with our higher natures and spiritual peace. Music that beats to primitive rhythms, hypnotic light displays, or deafening sound volumes leave it numb or mesmerized and in no way benefited. Because this touches on matters of taste, not everyone will agree with these observations, but they truly reflect what can be observed clairvoyantly. We need to pay much more attention to the nature of things we take in through our experience. The books we read, the movies we go to, the television we watch, the concerts we attend, and the recreation we participate in, all leave impressions on our astral bodies. Where these result in harm by disconnecting our contact with our higher nature we owe it to this emerging center of our awakening souls to protect and nurture its unfoldment.

Of all of our bodies, the astral vehicle is the weakest and most vulnerable, largely due to its attraction to stimulation and lack of discipline. When it is bored, restless and dissatisfied it seeks excitement. This immaturity must eventually give way to a valuing of serenity, beauty, and the uplift of God Spirit within. Training this vehicle to make this transition becomes our daily exercise. One important point about the astral body is its desire nature, for desire is its hallmark. Many eastern philosophies teach desirelessness, making the absence of this quality the aim of their path to enlightenment. Our Lord Christ, on the other hand, emphasized quite the opposite. Desire for Him was vital.

What made the difference was the kind of desire we are to cultivate. The Sermon on the Mount addresses the desire for a multitude of fulfillments that serve God and the spiritual life. For Him there were wise desires and those that were unwise. In the words of the Apostle Paul, *"And now abideth faith, hope, love, these three; but the greatest of these is love."* (I Cor 13:13) The Lord Christ's mission was a transformation of the planet: *"Thy kingdom come. Thy will be done in earth, as it is in heaven."* (Mat 6:10) Clearly, this concept of desire has nothing to do with physical pleasures, earthly power, or material wealth. Yet it is a keen longing, indeed a quest, a seeking out that sets us in motion such that we become doers of the Word, going about our Father's business with holy enthusiasm.

One of the most important things for the emotional body to exercise is affection — genuine demonstrated affection. Too many of us, though we care, allow a wall of reserve to stand between ourselves and others. We must remove that wall and in its place express our caring. This caring should include not just people but our pets, the birds that visit our yards, and all of life. We should communicate our affection broadly and spontaneously. Even when walking down the street passing people we don't personally know, we should find ways to acknowledge their importance and signal that we care.

There are people whose faces show a hollowness or sadness within. Find ways to light up their eyes by revealing that you care. Make sure that your love for others is more than in your mind. Engage your emotions because when your caring comes from there it rings true and lifts the spirit of the other person. You will discover that to touch someone in this way, to look at them such that you know how important they are, returns a heartwarming blessing.

Again, break your habit of reserve. It is time to speak and to act — to do whatever it takes to demonstrate how much you love others in the manner that our Lord exemplified. Listen to your own emotions indicating what has been neglected in the lives of others, and what needs to be lifted. Discover love's transforming power to change how you feel, how you think, how you see. If you find yourself discouraged, do something that lights up another's life. Look for something that invites enthusiasm, that awakens appreciation. Go about your day on the wings of the Holy Spirit knowing that in this one's eyes there is only beauty and wonder. You will be at peace within.

Know that your astral body can grow — that its wounds can heal. Realize that all wrong attitudes, all prejudices, create on this body what resemble blisters. If these become agitated they can actually tear open a hole in the aura, resulting in a significant loss of physical and emotional energy. In time, these gashes heal but often not without leaving us struggling with a sense of emptiness or depression. It is important that we backtrack at this point and reconstruct how we allowed ourselves to end up in such a situation. We need to ensure that we avoid such missteps in the future.

As we are mortal humans, not everything in our lives is happy or smooth, nor is it intended to be. We have our debts to pay, our karma to meet, and as we are not yet perfect we will face new lessons and encounter more testings. In the classroom of life not all of these will be easy. What counts, however, is our response, our attitude. Let it be with enthusiasm and engagement. Let us be engrossed in what each day sets before us — the responsibilities that fall to us, the relationships that are ours to unfold, and the opportunities that abound all about us. Appreciate life. Enjoy it. As we do, our astral body will blossom and be beautiful to behold. For one who is clairvoyant, it will be seen to have a sheen intermingling peach with gold, for these are the colors of spiritual joy and contentment. It is a radiance the Angels themselves know when they experience the same joyous feeling.

One of the most disturbing things we can bring upon ourselves is to get behind schedule for some important engagement or obligation and then find ourselves hurrying. We become impatient, irritable, and accident-prone.

How can we regain our composure, other than to resolve to arise an hour earlier when next faced with this situation? Who is to guide us through all of this training? The Lord Christ, of course, who is our wayshower.

Recall the words of the psalmist David, who was our Lord in his former life: *"He will lead me beside the still waters."* (Ps 23:2) Pause for a moment and envision the deep waters of a tranquil lake and feel your agitation coming to rest. *"He restoreth my soul."* (Ps 23:3)

We must put our souls in command of this moment and feel the peace of God that passes all understanding, at last in charge. If we do this, we will have taken a decisive step toward the mastery of our wayward emotions.

Chapter 4
The Mental Body

The mental body stands in a most interesting contrast to the astral body. It has a more varied range of available talents and resources to draw from. It is also more objective and balanced in its perspectives, as well as being a richer source of inspiration. The latter comes about because both the etheric and astral bodies are more grounded, while the mind has access to vision, intuition, and creativity. In addition, the mind is the seat of our intelligence, our memory, our analytical skills, and our cognitive abilities. A great part of our progress in life depends on our capacity to recognize and solve problems — an activity for which the mind is best suited.

There is also a difference between the mental and astral bodies in their clairvoyant appearance. The astral body is the most colorful of all the bodies, spanning the rainbow and most notably preferring bright hues. The mental body, on the other hand, favors pastel hues which suit its more reflective and dispassionate view of the world.

As with the other lower bodies, the mind follows closely the outline of the physical form. In appearance, what gives it distinction is the presence of its seven chakras which distribute energy in such a way that it resembles a container of boiling water. The surface of this vehicle is full of constant undulations corresponding to the activity of thought forms being released by the individual's mental processes. When we are contemplating an ideal, something that looks like colorful vapors drifts outwards from the center of ourselves. It is quite fascinating to observe. Altogether, the energies of this body are more refined and flexible than the other bodies reviewed thus far; they certainly move more rapidly.

There are interesting differences between the astral and mental bodies at the level of consciousness as well. We consciously contact people according to the plane in which we are most interested and comfortable, and therefore more active. We function in the astral plane when we think personally and fondly of another individual. That might be a loved child, our mother, or a close friend. We look at those relationships quite subjectively in terms of how we feel at that moment and how we experience our connection with them.

When we are very interested in someone, but our viewpoint in consciousness is more analytical and oriented toward understanding that person, we are operating in the mental plane. Moreover, our prayer or meditation work will also reflect one plane or the other, depending again on how we relate to this individual.

There is no set rule of thumb pertaining to the size of the mental body's emanation. It will expand quite suddenly when it experiences the joy of insight or revelation, but in its more typical mode of operation, one of quiet reflection and analysis, its emanations might extend from three to eight inches. When it consistently extends much beyond that range we are very likely observing a genius. On the other hand, the mental aura of almost anyone is capable of a momentary expansion when there is a sudden burst of realization or inspiration.

The mental body is particularly suited for meditation since it is capable of expanding and quickening its energies as the occasion invites. What is expanding is not the mental body itself but the wavelengths of mental essence that course through it as one thinks or realizes. Meditation itself, when the individual is uplifted and in touch with the higher frequencies of consciousness, brings a sense of oneness with God through a distinct awareness of being transported into a new dimension of existence, leaving one with a longing to return. Of course, meditation can be more perfunctory and dutiful, much like a routine mental exercise, just as it can be lost altogether in the struggle to keep the mind from wandering aimlessly. Clairvoyantly, however, it is the soul which brings us across the threshold of higher consciousness, opening the gates of our minds to illumination and transformation.

However, a reverse process may also occur. The emanations of the mental body shrink whenever we encounter a repellent situation or one that arouses a strong negative atmosphere such as fear, anger, or worry. When these circumstances appear, it is a signal to address these unwelcome intruders directly, turning them around by whatever means it takes. Otherwise, like an untreated virus, they spread throughout our system, and can bring us to our knees unless we take corrective action.

In its natural mode, the mental body is quite lovely, radiating its pastel shades of color alongside the astral body's use of rich, bright colors. More tranquil and reflective, the mind nevertheless interacts with its astral neighbor. If you should be striving toward wholeness, for example, every thought along these lines will display a color that is a more subdued expression of its astral companion's more vivid hue.

If you are strongly focused in your mental activity, as in prayer or meditation or in solving a challenging problem, the entire aura responds. Because the auric emanations are porous, there is a blending of energy from the etheric through the mental and beyond, when we are highly attuned or creatively engaged in mental pursuits. At such times the participation of the upper triad (soul, adonai, and monad) has yet to be noticeably significant. Its strength, sufficient to be consciously experienced, awaits future unfoldment. Still, its influence is felt, but for most humans it is the upper reaches of the mental body that form the boundary of what we can consciously attain and comprehend. While it may seem disappointing not to have clear contact with one's soul, this is actually a very good achievement, considering that the higher mental levels are quite engaging and intuitively insightful. The average person very probably would think he or she had reached the soul. Of course, when consciousness eventually breaks through to this lofty region, the difference is unmistakable, as we will see when that body is next described.

The radiations from the mental body are primarily yellow. As we think about different topics, however, other colors come into play. If we are pleasantly reminiscing about the past, lavender tends to take over the mental emanations. If we are contemplating the Angel Kingdom as Christmas approaches, beautiful light blue currents mingle with the yellow. An individual who is scientific and practical, who is slow and deliberate in making decisions, will have a great deal of ochre or orange-yellow in his or her mental body.

When we allow worrisome thoughts to enter our minds, the yellow gives way to a grey overcast. If we are thinking selfishly about some situation, the aura will have a brown emanation. All that it takes to bring the aura back to a lovely clear yellow tone is to occupy the mind with constructive and interesting thoughts requiring the exercise of our intelligence.

Once an individual awakens to a spiritual life, and takes on the responsibility of purifying and elevating his or her manner of living, the yellow in this one's mental body changes hue. It lightens and becomes clearer. This process continues to refine the aura until the third degree of initiation when the yellow in the aura is nearly indistinguishable from white itself.

One might ask how is the mental body vulnerable — what harms it? And the obvious answer is all the negative states are harmful because they cause this body to contract and if that isn't corrected it can bring about serious consequences. When the mind is preoccupied with fear, suspicion, possessiveness, self-pity, or depression, to mention only a few of such states, the mental body shrinks. At the same time it actually appears to be covered with a grey hood, so debilitating is this condition. It is most unpleasant to observe.

There are times when, even though free of negative thought forms ourselves, we might encounter them unexpectedly. A typical example would be passing a cocktail lounge or bar. What is so unpleasant about these settings is the presence of addictive entities that frequent such places — the monkey-like figure that clings to the back of an alcoholic is no mere hallucination. It exists as an actual presence from the lower astral plane and is a product of the mind's enslavement to alcohol. Another setting which is hard on the mental body's well-being is a darkened room where people nevertheless are awake but the vibrations are unconstructive. Here the darkness intensifies the low-grade atmosphere, fueling its negative thought forms. Bars and so-called "dens of iniquity," common within the drug culture, prefer this setting. Locations such as restaurants, for example, that have dimly lighted interiors, while not harmful, are not uplifting to the mind. They might be romantic or give a person a sense of privacy, but the mind prefers light. It thinks best in natural sunlight or in a well-illumined room. There are exceptions, of course, when we might be meditating in a darkened room, often with candlelight. What makes this conducive to the mind's quickening and sensitivity is its focus on the light within, in contrast to the darkened surroundings without. One looks within to experience illumination, and given this incentive and purpose, the mind is delighted. Meditation is particularly beneficial for the mind.

So much of life on earth demands our attention turned to its outer aspect, that the mental body has little opportunity to discover what awaits it deep within. But once we begin the experience of meditation and contemplation, we swiftly realize its potential for enlightenment. Once we taste enlightenment it becomes our all- consuming quest.

From time to time you would do well to ask yourself: How am I using my mental body? Am I satisfied with how it functions? Am I having problems with it? Or am I mentally lazy, neglecting its skills and talents? The mind is just as susceptible to illness as are the emotional, etheric, or physical vehicles. It, too, can become agitated and frustrated. What is needed to maintain health and balance is the wise selection of what it takes in and what it keeps out.

The thinker within each of us must be ever awake and alert to the quality of information to which it attends and allows entrance. Its chief foe, when testings come, is the personality self which has its own self-serving agenda — things it desires and things it resists. If its demands are followed, the thinker, striving for a higher set of goals, is outvoted and now the door of consciousness is open to the troubling mischief of this wayward element within us.

Until its wants and immaturity are overcome, the mind is in for a stormy ordeal. The answer is for the spiritual will of the struggling individual to come to his or her senses and take command, not aggressively or anxiously, but humbly and wisely changing course and keeping true to its destiny.

The mental body is indeed a wonderful vehicle. Its unfoldment depends on how good, how noble, and how intelligent we are willing for it to be. As mentioned previously, the mental, astral, etheric, and physical bodies do not continue with us into other lives. Only a seed atom from each of these vehicles is retained such that it forms the building block upon which a new and finer version of each vehicle will be recreated when next we return to the school of life.

In that return God gives us three gifts: life, individuality and consciousness. Of these three aspects, consciousness is the most important because the other two gifts from God — life and individuality — depend upon consciousness for their direction and unfoldment.

There are various kinds of consciousness. As a matter of fact, consciousness exists in every vehicle, but its easiest, most natural residence at this point of our evolution is the mental body. The time will come when the soul will be its favorite residence but, for most of us, that lies off in the future. We have an inner consciousness, which is subjective, and an outer consciousness, which is objective. We have a personal consciousness and an impersonal consciousness. Of particular interest to the mental body, we also have horizontal consciousness and vertical consciousness. Horizontal consciousness was most prominent in our earlier incarnations when we were still getting acquainted with the outer world and all of its interesting contents, events and relationships. It dealt with the variety of things known such as material interests, matters of the workaday world, and family life. As its name implies, its preoccupation is with the surface of life, with little attention to depth, as if all of our knowledge and experience were on a common level.

Vertical consciousness, on the other hand, addresses the inner nature of what we know and on what level its consciousness lies. As consciousness rises through each of our vehicles, it eventually ranges from the physical plane all the way to the monadic. While the latter is beyond our present capacity to reach, it nevertheless defines what lies before us as the vertical dimension of consciousness unfolds.

Vertical consciousness begins with an initial interest in philosophical or spiritual involvement and moral conduct. It rises from there into the metaphysical point of view emphasizing the power of free will to change ourselves and our circumstances. From there we pass into the esoteric realm of understanding where at last we know the plan of life and many of what were previously its mysteries. At this stage, we are awake to and perceptive of inner reality, and we are trained sufficiently to trust our insights and the revelations that come to us through our expanding and uplifted consciousness.

Finally, we come to the level of mysticism. Built on the foundations of the esoteric outlook which formed the most enlightened perspective of truth to this point, mystical consciousness takes us up to the last stage of conscious evolution. It is synonymous with cosmic consciousness. It is the experience of our souls — our higher selves — at last in command. It is pure, illumined, and linked unbrokenly to God.

True mystics are never wordy, for they realize truth itself is simple and clear. In their eyes everything is reduced to essences — to succinct observations. As these revelations eventually find their way into the minds of mystics, they begin to unravel their implications and the details emerge because the mind is geared to analyze and discover implications.

On the side of caution, there are a number of conditions that can compromise a healthy mind; we need to be aware of their nature and how to cope with their effects. Indecision and conflict, to begin with, are very stressful for the mind.

They create what appear to be crosscurrents in the aura that come about in gusts, causing the aura to form uneven lumps wherever the uncertainty arises. This is particularly complicated when the conflict is between rival functions located in the left and right hemispheres of the brain. Indecision and conflict result from a weakness of the will. For whatever reason, whether the person in question is trying to please everyone or simply can't face the responsibility of taking a stand, it is the will that must be strengthened. A good beginning exercise would be reading books or taking courses in management and decision-making. Ultimately, this individual must take the bull by the horns and acquire the skill by putting it into practice. It would also be well to obtain counseling to better understand the source of these indecisions or conflicts and how to address them.

Another disturbing condition is rigidity. When a person is unable to shift freely between alternative attitudes or modes of conduct, and develops a one-sidedness that is noticeable to others, he or she becomes defensive and the rigidity increases. When this occurs, the mental emanation in the aura becomes very dense. In addition, instead of being a lovely spheroid shape, it takes on the outlines of a cube. Unless this changes, the onset of mental illness is not far away. For all three of these troublesome characteristics, one response that is essential is the reversal of one's thinking processes. This must take place promptly and diligently. It is especially important to talk to your mental body. When confronted with a hurt or disappointment that has you feeling sorry for yourself, try speaking in this manner: "Dear God, open my mind and clear it of all pain and self-pity. Help me to see that what this shows me is a weakness that needs overcoming and if I follow through I will be free of its hold — and that is a great blessing in Christ's Name." Of the four lower vehicles that form the square supporting the upper triad, the mental body is the most responsive to constructive change; so it pays to exercise this attribute.

Among the things that are best for the mind are its needs for variety and challenge. Too many people allow their minds to follow narrow ruts of thinking rather than choosing a broad spectrum of mental pathways. Frequently introduce new problems for it to solve and new creations to envision. Take up chess or word games, read articles and books that present new technology or the results of scientific research, and if you are a parent, investigate the new frontiers of educational practice. The mind loves to explore fresh topics and invent logical arguments in favor of what it sees as right or against what it sees as wrong. Keep informed and abreast of developments in a variety of fields and your mind will stay forever young.

Another practice that engages the mind is the ability to organize and keep track of information. This avoids mental scatteredness and laziness. You might wish to create shopping lists in your mind, devising new ways to recall all items. As a check, you would do well to carry with you a written list to verify the accuracy of your memory; but the key is engaging your mind and keeping it agile. This is also especially useful in giving talks — to memorize and work from an outline so that you speak freely and spontaneously.

What is most important in the use of our minds is the ability to concentrate and keep focused. This is vital in the art of meditation. The number one complaint of those new to this practice is that their minds wander rather than hold true to the intended subject. The mental discipline that concentration involves is being able to follow a line of thought from its inception to its conclusion with deliberation and without deviation. As one progresses with this ability it allows the individual to practice concentration in the midst of distractions and competing activities. Once achieved, it soon proves itself to be a valued asset.

When dealing with the mind there is always the risk of getting lost in a labyrinth of details that, in the end, are useless. Such a condition leads one into a very mediocre state of mind that sheds little if any light in the thinker's mind or the minds of those he or she addresses or contacts. When such individuals tire of this uninspired mental boredom and find themselves in nature and receptive to the loftier vibrations that this realm offers, these trifling preoccupations disappear and the door to genuine enlightenment opens. It is an adventure in signs and symbols, just as all nature mystics have revealed—writers such as John Muir and Henry David Thoreau—it is a never-ending story, ever unfolding.

As with all things that form the path of discipleship, balance is important. Concentration should not become so dominating that it shuts out your contact with other duties or needs. One way to accomplish this is to place time boundaries on its exercise such that after a half hour or so, you shift to other endeavors that allow access to your field of attention. This is especially timely when the needs of other people come into play. In the case of meditation itself, that is an ideal span of time to devote the mind to its practice. Longer periods may lead to an imbalance in development and an avoidance of important matters in the outer world and our relationships and responsibilities therein. Again, it is a balance that must be struck if we are to fulfill the wholeness of God's plan for us.

On the practical side, we need to channel the energies of our minds into useful pathways. We should be harnessing the mind's ability to organize, comprehend, and apply its insights into the wealth of information that comes its way. It was the psychologist William James who observed that we make use of perhaps only ten percent of the mind's potential. What an extraordinary reservoir of human talent and resources goes untapped!

One of these mental resources is envisioning—creating in the mind's eye a picture of what is to be, God willing. It is one of the most potent skills we can turn to for it forms an archetypal blueprint that, once grounded, manifests itself. Persons who are gifted in this way seem to possess a magic that attracts all manner of things. There is, however, a word of caution. The use of this power needs to be unselfish or it runs the risk of being abused. Its wisest use is not in attracting material goods but in setting the stage for enlightenment and transformation. The mind in this respect is a causative force: what you think about you tends to become. Thought, after all, is creative and what occupies your mind sets the stage for what follows.

Thus far, we have discussed the constructive use of this talent. In equal measure, if the mind is occupied with fear or anger, it will attract that burden as well. We need constantly to monitor what gains our attention and when we become aware of a preoccupation with worry or resentment or other negative states, it is time to do a turnabout. An excellent opportunity to make a fresh start comes when we begin a new job or meet new people who don't see us in terms of our past mistakes or shortcomings. What an excellent time it is to turn over a new leaf in our own outlook and conduct.

One of the mind's most selfish and damaging abuses is to use its powers to manipulate others—to get people to be what you want them to be or do what you want them to do—all for your own advantage. This tendency borders on black magic and must be rooted out at all costs. In fact, any misuse of one's will to gain favor or to win out over others is to enter upon a path of darkness. It is best counteracted by a commitment to integrity, encouragement, and the gift of friendship to all those who enter the circle of your influence.

In the same vein the mind heals. It does this by changing the viewpoints and the expectations of the person afflicted with disease or injury, anxiety or discouragement. Perhaps the individual tires of being afflicted and that makes for the cure. Other times it is a leap of faith that ends the stricken condition. Whatever enters the picture to transform how the person sees his or her situation, that is the beginning of the healing experience. What most speeds the process and carries the day are the qualities of love and compassion which a true healer caringly creates. And the more depth, specificity, and clarity that goes into this treatment, the more effective will be the patient's recovery.

As the mind can engage its energies to facilitate a cure, it can also disengage itself from a setting where unwholesome or unconstructive elements have accumulated — for instance the thought forms of disturbed individuals. This form of purposeful detachment is often the saving grace for a sensitive soul to endure the company of thoughtless, agitated people.

We need to constantly enrich and improve the quality of our thinking. Thought can purify and refine the atmosphere of a day, turning what otherwise would be an overcast of dull and dreary emanations into the sunlight of an illumined consciousness. Through thought we can visualize our ideals, form our goals, and draw closer to their attainment.

For all of its prestige among western minds, reason is a vastly overvalued discipline, a two-edged sword that cuts both ways, and leaves its practitioner more often stymied than enlightened. The truly creative gift of the mind is not argument but insight and intuition that leaps over the painstaking points of a rational analysis to the heartbeat of truth itself.

Consider the experience of meditation that is awake and alive—that lifts one into the presence of peace and ensoulment. We feel surcharged and wonderfully uplifted. Right there we have experienced the transforming power of thought that has taken place before our very eyes. We now can think more clearly and purely and the thinker within us can instruct us as never before, opening the gates of our minds to fresh currents of creativity that stream eternally from the Inner Worlds.

We have this thinker within us to intelligently guide us to our destiny this lifetime. Perhaps there is no more consequential act that the mental body serves, than the act of choice. Which way to turn when we come to a crossroads? What to do with our lives once we come of age? Which of the many opportunities life offers to grasp? All this, and all the while we're striving to keep in mind the little things in daily life that, in the end, add up to the major sum in our karmic accounts. Certainly, until we are soul-activated, soul-aware, and soul-inspired, living from the highest vantage point our minds possess is the most purposeful choice we can exercise. The mind is a much neglected tool, too often overlooked in favor of our preference for simply passing time or pursuing personal agendas. We need to ignite the energies of our chakras on the mental level of our being and take charge!

Two final thoughts. As our minds unfold and bring through impressions and insights, there is always the temptation to take personal credit for what comes to us. We will be wise to humbly give all credit to God from the start. And second, the more unselfishly, sincerely, and gratefully we can experience the mind's abilities, the more ably we can answer the question posed to David in the Old Testament—a question that awaits us all when we set foot on the path to God: *"Whither have ye made a road today?"* (I Samuel 27:10)

Chapter 5
The Soul—The Body of Light

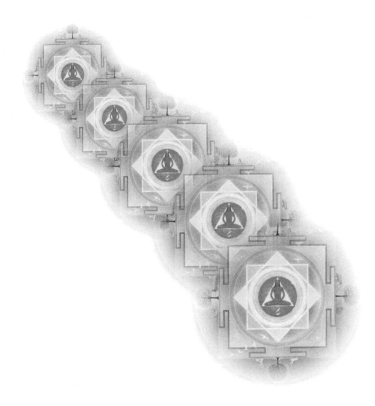

The awakening of the soul is an experience that has no equal in the journey Godward. After lifetimes of living in the shadowy passageways of one's lower bodies, the soul comes to us like the discovery of a new world—a magical world. Until this moment, we have pursued all manner of notions and preconceptions regarding God and the Inner Worlds. But what was missing was its actual experience. The soul gives us that. Once we behold its shining reality, we will never again be content with lesser realms.

Consciousness of the soul is not a common experience. It is quite likely that the vast majority of humanity in incarnation today will live out their lives without actually being aware of this jewel within them. At best, they will idealize it or unwisely mimic what they imagine to be its attributes when desiring to make an impression on someone. Many ministers undoubtedly find themselves caught in this dilemma before their congregations each week, role-playing what they sense their souls ought to be. Yet, when that time comes for the soul to break through the barricades of the personality self, revealing the pure joy of its illuminating presence, so transforming is this discovery that it comes like the gift of vision to one born blind.

Let us now speak about the attributes of the soul. The distance between the mental body and the soul is immense, for it is the soul which brings us to the upper triad of our being including itself, the adonai, and the monad or God Inbeing. These three centers are pure and undefiled and usher in the era of our unbroken contact with God. Of course this link with the Divine doesn't manifest overnight. It awakens gradually and often in moments when we least expect it. It communes with our consciousness in the language of inner perception—the immediate experience of God and the Inner Worlds.

While the mind at its highest levels operates with its own access to intuition that is quite creative and insightful, it is the soul which perfects this attribute with the emergence of inner perception and the sixth sense.

It is the nature of intuition that it manifests as a gift out of the blue in the form of an insight, a prompting, and impression or a realization. It can be visual, or language-based, much like a message or an illuminating observation. The word "insight" perhaps best captures its essence as it always reveals a truth or an awareness that makes a difference. It may solve a problem, call something overlooked to our attention, shed light on one of life's mysteries, or be the source of an act of creation or discovery, amounting to an ingenious revelation. On the other hand, it can be peculiarly illogical, ill-timed, or seemingly unimportant at the moment, but if ignored, it invariably proves itself correct. Moreover, as the language of the soul, intuition becomes our means of circumventing the personality self and linking consciousness to this source of wisdom that lies so deep within.

In appearance the soul is a body composed of a highly refined light. It is a larger body than the physical form and its properties are quite unique. When not active, as in the majority of the human population that is still spiritually unawakened, the soul takes the form of a mantle whose presence is nevertheless capable of making contact with us. However, when it is active in the awakened individual, it possesses direct knowledge. The soul is able to distinguish all sides of a situation. Details of knowledge are eliminated and only the essences of truth are retained in higher consciousness.

Composed of a resplendent opalescence, it gives off sparkling iridescent flashes as it signals its wise counsel to both our consciousness and unconsciousness. All the while it emits a soft luminous glow that gives it its name, the body of light. To one with clairvoyance, the soul of every person is wondrously beautiful. In the evolutionary scheme of life, the principal difference between individuals is the extent to which the soul is active in consciousness and conduct.

The descriptions thus far have been for an advanced soul. In the case of most persons, the soul, though still resplendent, is less prominent and much less active. Outer appearances of people are not reliable indications of what lies within. Persons whose personalities are difficult may nevertheless have that jewel within which is magnificent and free of negativity.

The soul expresses itself in essences. In place of a symphony that requires much time to play, on the causal plane this is reduced to a single melodious chord. In place of a lengthy poem, one striking phrase will sum up its meaning. And in place of a philosophical dissertation, a vibrant illuminating conclusion will be harvested by the soul. All the insights and elaboration follow intuitively — nothing is lost.

The soul works with lightning rapidity. Its perceptions and receptions are nearly instantaneous. Great works of art or brilliant inventions are frequently born in a flash. To capture their fleeting presence in consciousness is arduous, not because the soul's creativity puts us to the test so much as because our human minds labor so awkwardly.

We think of the causal world as the dimension wherein the Divine Spirit stores its creative and constructive powers. It is usually from this level that the transforming acts of redemption, regeneration, and revelation take place, descending into our consciousness as a gift from God.

The soul is our repository of this giftedness. This is so because its habitat is the causal plane where are stored all the inventions to be, all the wisdom yet to be revealed, along with the latent powers, capabilities, and creative endeavors the world has yet to see. When, in prayer and meditation, we draw close to our soul, we are aligning ourselves to be perceptive of its gifts. And unlike the mind which has to work diligently to think through to a solution or to formulate a plan, the soul does so in the blink of an eye.

Prophets and poets both speak in the language of the soul. Mystics and wayshowers of all religions have this same clarity of vision which penetrates barriers of time, custom and precedent.

Gifted writers, with concise and illumined imagery of Spirit, describe in truest language how the soul views life from its watchtower. When a poem or book is written from the height of soulic consciousness we are not able to improve on its wording whatsoever, try as we may.

The soul, then, is a luminous body, taller and more beautiful than anything in the physical world. Its consciousness possesses wisdom. Its gifts and powers are exceptional: when manifest in the outer world, these become rare talents. As with the other bodies before it, it possesses seven chakras or energy centers. Through these centers pass energy of an extraordinary kind, whose versatility and vitality opens the gates of consciousness to undreamed-of opportunities and realizations.

Upon death, permanent seed atoms from the physical, astral and mental bodies are stored in the heart chakra of the soul where they eventually will become the prototypes for our next incarnation. The time will come when we meet with the Kindel Archangel responsible for planning that incarnation. He helps the person choose the background and circumstances of our life to come.

The soul looks upon life as a long-term investment. It expects some losses in the beginning as its influence is muted but in the long run it foresees that the day will come when the balance will swing in its favor. All through a lifetime the soul mantles the personality self. Its potential far exceeds the force of a thousand personalities, so potent is this part of one's seven-fold being. When the soul is young in its emergence, the outer personality will be dominant because the higher self is still largely unawakened and ineffective. For a very long time the personality self leads a busy, worldly and indulgent life. Then a crossroad is reached and the individual is faced with a crisis or a sorrow that reveals the emptiness of this outer personality. At long last the earth pilgrim surrenders his or her will to the soul within and turns to God for help. This crucial act arouses the dormant soul bringing into play its superior wisdom and guidance. With the stirring of the soul, conscience, integrity and fine character will begin to develop.

As the personality self lessens its hold, the emerging soul makes the person more radiant and light-filled. The personality realizes that it has access to help which is imperishable and immortal. Now begins the purification of the personality. Its limited, prejudiced outlook surrenders to the spacious, universal and well-rounded concepts of the soul. Whenever we are irritated by the mannerisms of others, it is their personality traits that test us. The soul is never offensive; it is always relaxed, graceful, aware and reverent. What is vital to remember is, through our grasp of spiritual instruction, to put it into practice and transform our weaknesses into strengths and our doubts into certainties.

There is a story of a simple Canadian girl who married an Englishman following his visit to her village. In middle life he inherited an earldom. This meant a historic title and a high position. The humbly bred Canadian woman was no longer young, but with her husband she went to England to take up the duties for which she had no training. But such was her naturalness, her sincerity and her lack of affectation that she found friends and became beloved in one of the most complex and exacting societies in the world. It was her humility which carried her through. She demonstrated that there is but one aristocracy, the aristocracy of character and the transformation of consciousness that accompanies it.

The predominant characteristics of soulic consciousness are those of love, unity, wisdom, creativity and intuition. Soul consciousness is after all, Christ consciousness active in each of us. Whatever adds to the christing of our thoughts, emotions and acts brings the soul's transforming expression into and through us. A well-developed soul has a nature which is Christlike. Only motives and thoughts which are self-giving influence it, for it has never known a selfish wish or need. Such a soul has respect for the values of both small and great things, yet it is never burdened by responsibilities. When intuitions or inner experiences are authentic, they remain vividly in mind. Passing impulses or illusions fade away quickly and are forgotten. Evidence of extraordinary gifts or talents reveals what the soulic consciousness is capable of, for all truly great talent is an outflow of soulic powers.

On the causal plane the soul may communicate with Masters without the personality self being aware of it. It often contacts the inner selves of individuals with which it is familiar without the knowledge of normal consciousness. Draughts of these inner plane communions find their way into outer awareness later in the form of realizations or inspired revelations and we rejoice in receiving them.

All the sacred rites of the church are accompanied by the activities of the soul. At christening the soul radiates a new energy into the baby's aura, particularly its higher bodies. The chakras are activated during the ceremony and the Watcher or Guardian Angel appears and remains with the imprinting soul from that time forward. During this ceremony the soul connects with the entire seven-fold being of the infant, aligning all of its faculties to the monad or God Presence.

At communion, the soul becomes magnified when the bread and juice are taken. A divine force from the innermost realms flows out and quickens the entire person. An overshadowing of the Christ Spirit is distinctly realized when the minister says to each devotee, *"The Christ renews thee unto life eternal."*

A wedding is most inspiring to witness superphysically. While the couple repeat their vows, each of their souls glisten and gleam with brilliant white fire. After the minister says, *"Bless, O God, this ring, that he who gives it and she who wears it, may abide in Thy peace, remembering their vows unto life's end,"* a luminous circle mantles the hands of the couple. As the bridegroom says, *"With this ring I thee wed in the sight of God,"* a glorious blazing white Light shines over the couple. When the light is withdrawn the causal bodies of the couple have been united so that they appear as one.

The unfoldment of the soul forms the whole objective of incarnation. Each passing incarnation gives it greater definiteness and individuality, along with more awareness of realities which move behind the visible spheres.

Before we can become unbrokenly aware of our soul it is necessary that we purify, consecrate and redeem the physical body, etheric sheath, emotions and mind. It is these lower vehicles that have yet to be cleansed of the shadowlands which make our lives uncertain and at odds with our higher natures. The physical body needs to be free of weariness and illnesses. The etheric sheath needs recharging and renewal. The astral body requires freedom from our human overdesirousness and aversions. The mental body must be purified of selfish interests so it can be a vehicle of harmony and spiritual watchfulness. Until these lower bodies are cleansed they are impervious to the frequencies of the higher levels.

When the soul turns its full attention upon its lower vehicles, the change which it introduces yields a remarkable effect. With this channeling, we become conscious of a new energy and presence at work in our life. It is essential to appreciate the significance of this awakening influence in the transforming of consciousness and the cultivation of character for it marks the onset of our life as a disciple — a life that will free us from the pains and passions of the personality self.

How often during a day do we think of our souls? We should form the habit of looking up and within to this body of light frequently throughout each day. Within the boundaries of our earthly evolution it is unlimited and immortal. The more we turn our attention to this higher self, the more we will be refreshed and helped by its superior vitalizing and enlightening wisdom. We should ask questions of our souls and patiently await the answers being flashed back into our objective consciousness.

Most persons come upon times when communication with this higher aspect within is natural and spontaneous. We feel inspired and enriched. This is the time when we should use a spiritual journal to record as best we can what was received. These journal entries might vary from inner promptings that fine-tune the conduct of our lives to direct contacts with our Guardian Angels or great inner teachers. For the most part, however, these receptions will be aimed at the little steps of growth that each day places before us. Because these opportunities form the stepping stones of daily progress, we should be filled with gratitude and joy.

In the quest for God, the soul gives us the incentive and the energy to so strive. Not only is it the source of our higher aspirations, it is also the means of overcoming the resistance and rebellion of the shadow, that dark side of the personality self ruled by instinct gratification. In fact, it is the opposition of the lower nature within each of us that tests us to our limits. In this paradoxical manner, like an inexperienced but determined mountain climber, we gradually gain our skills, wisdom, conditioning and perseverance.

It is vital that we appreciate early in this greatest of adventures, the psychology of the shadow — that any event drawing us closer to the light is profoundly threatening to our dark side. It is axiomatic that whenever we make a spiritual vow that involves the soul, and conscientiously pursue it, the shadow will respond for the sake of its own survival. Its stratagems are classic. One of its most successful is simply to lure us into neglecting our vows altogether. Failing that, it fashions a series of tests designed to compromise our efforts, discourage us, or otherwise undermine our resolve.

It is in these engagements that we discover the resources our soul possesses to outwit and outlast the shadow. In this confrontation it was the shadow to which the Apostle Paul referred when he said, *"The good that I would, I do not; and the evil that I would not, that I do."* (Rom 7:19) In another context, however, he was speaking of the soul when he said, *"I live, yet not I, but Christ liveth in me."* (Gal 2:20) And so it is that while the shadow is incorrigible, the soul is unconquerable and prevails in the end. That is how the Creator has designed the course of human evolution—the archetypal duel between good and evil within each individual.

Every person is much more than he or she appears to be. In looking at a friend physically we see less than one thousandth of what that person is. The mirrors of our minds reflect only a small percentage of what lies beneath the surface. The greater part of what lies hidden is the seedbed of Divinity which awaits our own awakening.

When we are able to raise our consciousness to the level of the higher self, the helpfulness of the soul becomes immediately available. The soul, once we make its contact, always yearns and strives upward, slowly transcending the burdens of the lower bodies which stand in the way. What is called a lifetime on earth is to the soul but a single day of school. Those who possess soulic consciousness are able to rectify their karma intentionally; for these individuals, very much good is possible and very much achievement is attainable.

Chapter 6
The Adonai

Of the seven bodies making up an individual's being, the least is known about the adonai. It, along with the soul and God Spirit Indwelling, form the upper triad — that part of us that is divinely pristine and pure in contrast to the four-square base of the lower bodies.

The soul marks the beginning of our higher nature and, given its greater accessibility to consciousness, functions for many lifetimes as our real self. However, it is the adonai that ultimately becomes our true identity. Its two principal attributes are our divine and unique individuality and the center of our spiritual will.

Whenever we find in sacred literature the pronouncements "I am. . ." or "I will. . ." we can be certain they pertain to these two functions of the adonai. Because so little has been written about its existence, it remains wrapped in mystery. Still, glimpses of its nature have been revealed. Along with its expression of identity and spiritual will, it serves as a well-spring of wisdom, intoning the energies of purity and power. It is a most wondrous vehicle.

Its outshining of truth is condensed to essences. A characteristic revelation would be the verse, "*Arise, shine; for thy Light is come, and the glory of the Lord is risen upon thee.*" (Isa. 60:1) Moreover, whenever we see the title *Lord* in sacred scripture, it is the signature of the adonai. The phrase "God in us" on the other hand, identifies the God Spirit or God Indwelling.

A further clue as to the presence of this noble aspect is the appearance of the word *now* for it signals the adonai's will that we must be about our Father's business without delay.

To harvest the spiritual bounty the adonai offers us, we need to address its faculty of spiritual will. The quality that we humans most lack in our quest for God is steadfastness, perseverance, and the determination to live the life and follow the way. We are so easily distracted, so quickly discouraged, so prone to procrastinate when it comes to our choice between serving self or serving God, that until this capability is realized, we are like a whisper lost in the wind.

We acquire this will by turning our attention inward and visualizing the abundance of will the adonai commands. Prayerfully, we see this reservoir of determination and perseverance connected to our need for self-conquest on the one hand and enlightenment on the other. In our meditations and remembrances, we observe the adonai's will coming actively into consciousness and permeating every atom of our being until we feel its presence on all levels of our existence.

In reaching an awareness of the adonai, we also have reached a critical threshold, for it is now that we must ask to be mantled so that no distraction, no discouragement, no procrastination be allowed to interfere with the flow of Divine Will now permeating our entire being. Envision the light of this will invading every vehicle of our totality.

What makes this such an important step is the inevitable response of the dark side of our personalities whenever we strive toward the light, and the light flowing through the adonai is extraordinary. We wisely surround ourselves with a triple ring-pass-not of the Christ light to safeguard our invoking the adonai.

There remain a few additional observations involving this vital aspect of our totality. Being the seat of our spiritual will, the adonai is the source to call upon to strengthen and refine that attribute as it is needed in our day to day opportunities. The role of the will gains prominence as we ascend the spiritual path. Central to its exercise is the discipline of choice. It is essential to be fully conscious of the times in a day when choices are taking place. So many of our choices occur unconsciously out of habit, and these are most often the ones needing transformation. In this sense, the adonai serves as a co-creator with God Inbeing.

In matters of healing, it is important to call upon the adonai as the Divine Self residing in the one seeking healing, to exert its archetypal well-being such that the affliction is replaced by its Divine counterpart.

The adonai is crystalline or diamond-like in appearance, reflecting the gloriously transcendent, blazing light that comes from the God Indwelling or seventh aspect of being just beyond it. The symbol for the adonai is the all-seeing eye. The adonaic realm duplicates everything that is active in the soulic region, only with greater intensity. From its lofty position it sends forth waves of strength, wisdom, power, and will. You can be sure whenever a transformation or healing becomes permanent, it has passed through and received the blessing of the adonai. And as the adonai is our lordly self, present and active when we have obtained mastery, the God-flame within us is destined to become our Logos in some distant eon.

It is no wonder then that in his retreat in Switzerland, Carl Jung had a sign with these words of Erasmus: *"Invoked or not invoked, God is present."*

Chapter 7
The Monad

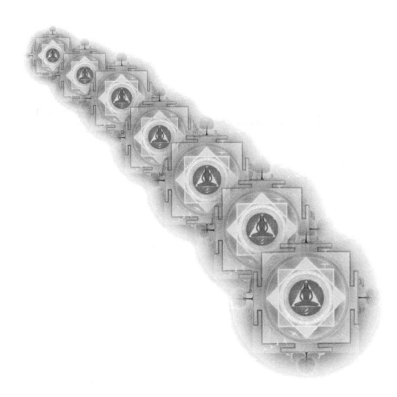

The greatest of quests is the quest for God. It is the supreme mission of life—the underlying purpose for which we exist and the aim of evolution carrying us inevitably towards its attainment. Connecting us to this destiny is the divine spark within known as the God-flame, the monad, God-Inbeing. It is the seed of our own *latent* Divinity. Like the seed of a giant sequoia tree, its active role in our destiny is eons away from fulfillment, but its presence here and now defines our future. While its force is minimal, awaiting our gradual ascent up life's initiatory pathway, it nevertheless unites us with our Creator and is our principal means of alignment with God the Whole.

The term "latent" is highlighted because some metaphysical teachers present this aspect of our being as if it were fully functioning at that level now when in fact these Godly powers are mostly dormant. What it can do currently is to be the communication link with God the whole, allowing us to invoke and invite these divine forces through meditation and prayer. It is a distinction that recognizes the prevalence of our egos, ever the obstacles between God and our personalities. It would be the height of absurdity to confuse an overreaching ambition to be perfect with the reality of a destiny far distant in our future.

In our personality selves we are mortal. Our physical, etheric, astral, and mental bodies do not possess everlasting life. Each of these vehicles experiences death, and when we incarnate on earth again we return with new vestments for each of those four lower bodies.

However, there is much in us which is immortal, relatively speaking. In addition to the faculties mentioned, we possess a causal body, an adonaic sheath and the form of our Invincible Presence who is Lord God Indwelling. From the time that we were individualized as human beings, we were given a soul and a body of light to serve the deathless and eternal God Spirit who is our inner regent in attunement with divinity.

Just as our physical form along with our energies, feelings, and thoughts evolve across incarnations, so shall we experience the superphysical awakening of our soul, adonai and God-presence as these come into the control and perfection of our sevenfold being. The time comes when we will be finished with our normal human progress and we begin the unfoldment of superconsciousness and its enlightening regime of training. At this juncture we are entering the final stages of our earthly evolution bringing about the transformation of our interests, ideals, and strivings. Most consequential of all, we will then have increasing access to the Inner Worlds and all of its resources.

Because the vehicles forming the upper triad are never at odds with one another, there is a harmony and reciprocity that is fresh and highly purposeful, accelerating the individual's progress. With the lower four vehicles we have to deal with an unpredictable mixture of human reactions ranging from resentment to admiration.

The monad or God Spirit within—our invincible self—is the only one of the sevenfold vehicles that endures forever. Even the soul and the adonai ultimately are no longer necessary, leaving only that which was forever divine within us to exist. Such a destiny is so far beyond our comprehension that it remains a matter of mystery and faith.

It has been mentioned previously that we come into each incarnation with newly created physical, etheric, astral, and mental bodies. In fact, what actually occurs is that at our death in the previous incarnation, a tiny permanent atom from each of the lower four vehicles is stored in our causal body in the region behind the heart chakra. Each of these permanent atoms contains a microscopic record of the important events that we experienced in each of the four vehicles. When the season arrives for us to be born once again on the earth, these seed atoms are utilized to act as magnets attracting essences from each level for the building of new bodies. The less advanced the individual, the more Angels assist in determining the development of the nucleus. The more advanced the soul, the more fully he or she plans the forthcoming incarnation.

Because the upper triad is so harmoniously linked together, it is natural to think of the soul, the adonai and the monad, as if these formed a unified structure of equal units. This would be most misleading since God Inbeing is singularly the greatest reality we contain. It is our immediate and direct contact with God the Whole. It is the only aspect of our sevenfold nature that will exist forever. In a word, it is *unique*.

Although this chapter began with a caution that because God is part of us, it does not mean we ourselves are therefore perfect, it would be equally incorrect to view God as remote and inaccessible. The threshold of God lies within each of us contained in God Inbeing. It is this seventh aspect of our being that patiently awaits our exercising at-one-ment.

In your morning meditation, after visualizing each of the seven vehicles, intone the phrase *God Inbeing* following the invocation of the powers of the Holy Trinity. As this realization blossoms in your consciousness, pause and visualize its immensity and potency, for this connection is infinite and timeless.

You might ask, how will I sense God within? First, you must practice the strong awareness of reverent recognition by actually sensing the awesome presence of God stirring in consciousness. Feel its energies rhythmically pulsing with each heartbeat. Second, through desire, aspiration and veneration you must pray before the altar of God Inbeing. Sense God's presence as a sea of light in which you are immersed. It is your Holy of Holies Indwelling—the self of light which completely enfolds you easily and deeply. Nor is it apart from you in any way, for it surrounds and assumes the natural contour and shape of your body positions.

Third, speak to your God self with new veneration and inclusion each day. For example, *"O God Inbeing, holy and wise art Thou. Send into all of me the raying of Thy light, the blessing of Thy spirit, the transforming of Thy power. Help me to become conscious of Thee forevermore, and to channel forth Thy mysteries in quietness and in reverence. Through Thy holy presence indwelling, thus shall it be."*

Fourth, each new day you will spend a few minutes in creative contemplation of this God force within you. It is important to remember that this God-flame, composed of individual form, is a complete replica in power, intelligence and divinity, of God the Whole. Through the means of God Inbeing, the whole of divinity blesses, inspires, and enlightens you.

Fifth, focus next on the regeneration and perfecting of being through the spiritualizing, the governing and the uplifting of the velocities or states of vibration of every vehicle belonging to your total being. To accomplish this you will wait, through one-pointed desire, upon the benedictions of God Inbeing energizing all of its vehicles of expression from the adonai downwards. In invoking this benediction from God Indwelling, you must desire, as each body is remembered, Deity's fullest penetration and healing of the faculty considered.

Then in rhythmic remembrances throughout a day, focus on God Inbeing's acceleration of the life current. On another occasion address the vehicle of individuality, the adonai, asking God Inbeing within you to consciously bless its whole faculty of Divine will. If it has been weak, remember to ask for a greater degree of will empowerment.

Concerning the faculty of the soul, seek a strengthening and an appointing of soul gifts of energies that would benefit from such treatment. If your intuitional abilities, for example, are too weak, devote a morning's endeavor to their quickening.

On another day you might concentrate on your creative endowments, increasing the fires of creativity through the empowerment of God Inbeing.

At least once a week from your mental realm earthward, treat specifically for the archetype of health to ray out through God Inbeing. Ask for God's health on the mental plane to become vigorous, improving your qualities of discernment, deduction, cognition, memory, and associated aspects of divine intelligence.

On the astral level, still focusing on the archetype of health, ask that the health inherent in God Inbeing be reflected throughout your emotional body. Deliberately and thoroughly, realize the qualities of harmony, refinement, strengthening, purification, and enrichment manifesting in your astral capabilities.

In like manner, visualize the broadcasting of cleansing, renewing and health-giving currents throughout your etheric vehicle. See these energies being contained and insulated in the name of God Inbeing.

An entire treatment period needs to be devoted to God Inbeing's infusion throughout your physical body of health-giving currents of revitalization. Whenever known organs require perfecting, in a relaxed and peaceful state of mind, let the influence of God Inbeing, which far exceeds x-ray ability, penetrate each given organ. Slowly and deliberately, in reverent attunement, emphasizing the personal pronoun "my," say, for example:

"God Inbeing, let your light empowerments ray through my lungs."

In like manner pronounce the intervention of God Presence to ground divine powers in those matters that challenge you, such as your relationships with others, business responsibilities, or personal crises. Invite, greet, trust, and honor the splendid God Self which is within you.

God Inbeing is composed of the light of God and consists of the equivalent of intelligence, will, love, and motion. Divine intelligence is reflected in your own individual mind. Divine will appears as your intentions. Divine love, so intrinsic to your inner Godhood, becomes the world of your feeling. Divine motion ensures that all of these attributes will be active rather than passive.

These four qualities together form the dimensions to call upon when you are challenged, tested or given the opportunity for new growth. God Indwelling is your richest source of constructive power to call upon as often as needed. As the need for each quality comes to your attention, call upon its divine presence to manifest in the situation before you, invoking its potent energies to transform your abilities to meet the demands confronting you. Be aware of the God quality entering your own being, engaging your resourcefulness and responsiveness. Visualize the constructive transformation that follows.

The God Self within cannot assume government of its reflected components until the lower reflections of these components are awakened, quickened and filled with the desire for this vertical linkage and the life-changing influences it brings. No force of intelligence is as near or as immediately effective as your individual God. When in the throes of testing, or on the crest of a great emotion, remember that the divinity that lies within you is the most available and answerable for your immediate, urgent needs.

In envisioning your God Indwelling, do not underestimate its true size or see it as a flame of vague proportions. It is larger and far more luminous than any other aspect of yourself. This God Spirit is the one part of your sevenfold being that will exist forever. Never for one moment has it experienced separation from the source of all that is.

All that you are, whether it be much or little, is the result of your contact with the Indwelling God. If your connection with this divine source within you has been feeble for lack of interest or lack of faith, the result may be a body lacking health and vigor, or a spirit lacking will or direction. Such a life gives the appearance of a weak desire to deal with outer reality, causing a disconnection with the wealth of opportunities that life on earth offers in abundance.

To cope with this sense of withdrawal from the school of life, it is vital to first mount a campaign to awaken your entire being to life's wealth of resources and circumstances that will enrich the transformation of your mind, your heart, and your awareness of the God Spirit within. Second, in spiritual patience await and consciously receive the benefits of its mantling. Third, invite and welcome the quickening forces which flow from the experience known inwardly as the *Great Out-*

shining. It is in this state that the government of God Indwelling becomes a realized aspect of your own selfhood.

Recall frequently in meditation how God Inbeing is of Logos potential and how it is affiliated with every developed Logos in the Kingdom of God. It is a connectedness with the entire universe and the divine manner and rule of all that is. Though this awareness is beyond our comprehension in most of its particulars, its presence is felt and experienced. To whatever extent we are able to fathom the immensity of God forces that govern creation, we should honor that awareness and, through this opening, appreciate its ongoing revelations.

Remember, when in ill health, that in order to correct incompleteness and limitation of any type, you must first go within to receive the positive attention and recognition from your own God Within. Because it possesses the hyper-intuitional faculty, it will, through the instrumentality of your prayers, align you with the appropriate source of divine wisdom.

You contain the splendor and all the aspects of God. Now, through your willingness and control, let them shine forth.

Chapter 8
The Seven Sacred Chakras

Intimately integrated with the seven bodies are the seven major chakras. As stated earlier, chakra is a Sanskrit word meaning wheel. It is called that because each of the seven chakras is wheel-shaped and constantly whirling around its hub. Their joint purpose is to provide the energy necessary for all the needs of our seven-fold being. These life force centers first manifest in the etheric body which, in turn, supplies the energy needs of the physical vehicle. Although the physical vehicle lacks chakras, it possesses organs and glands in their place which ground the energy flow coming from the etheric chakras. In addition to manifesting on the etheric level, chakras supply energy to each of the remaining bodies, as each body serves a specific function with its own energy requirements.

Thus, there are seven chakras and each chakra serves at six different levels corresponding to each of the six bodies beyond the physical. Energy supplied to the mental body, for example, is not the same as what is supplied to the astral body. And it is through the alignment of these seven chakras that we experience alignment throughout our sevenfold being. Briefly, they include the following:

1. *The root chakra*—base of the spine
2. *The spleen chakra*—spleen
3. *The navel or solar plexus chakra*—navel
4. *The heart chakra*—heart
5. *The throat chakra*—throat
6. *The brow chakra*—brow
7. *The crown chakra*—crown of the head

Each chakra is saucer-like rather than perfectly flat, with a body that reflects this concave image, and each has a hub from which extend lines of force resembling the spokes of a wheel which, in a healthy individual, rotate in a clockwise direction. In young souls these centers are about two inches across. As individuals evolve, these centers expand, reaching a width of twelve or more inches.

Besides supplying the energy for every human's daily needs, the higher chakras perform a unique service. They are the means of opening up our access to the Inner Worlds. Beginning with the heart chakra, each of these centers serves a vital function that directly draws us closer to God. Indeed, the word referring to the chakras in both the Old and New Testaments is "gate." The Bible verse that most pointedly confirms this is, *"Lift up your heads, O ye gates, and be ye lifted up, ye everlasting doors, that the King of Glory may come in."* (Ps 24:7) What fulfills this verse is the fact that the seventh body containing its chakras is the monad or God Spirit Indwelling. Not until we are approaching mastery do these divine energies awaken.

The spinal column serves as the rod of power under the direction of the God Self symbolized by the caduceus—the staff of a herald or physician—represented by the figures of two winged snakes entwined together. It contains primal energy which comes from God Supreme and courses down the spinal column. There are two other sources of energy that feed into the chakras. Vitality energy comes from the Solar Logos and flows up the right side of the spinal column; streaming up its left side is the kundalini fire originating with the Planetary Logos. All three energies enter through the gates of the seven chakras for each of our several bodies, an inflowing that is wonderful to observe clairvoyantly. These three forces: the primal or God force, the vitality force and the kundalini force provide the fuel, so to speak, that is necessary for us to undertake our evolutionary journey up the Mountain of God.

The first of these energy centers is the *root chakra* located at the base of the spine. It radiates the colors red and orange and has four spokes. On the etheric level its principal function is procreation, served through the sex drive which incites energy for that purpose. It is the lowest expression of the kundalini fire that travels the length of the spinal cord. This vital force, coming from the Planetary Logos, originates in the center of the earth and, like radium, can be constructive or destructive. The difficulties encountered when this instinctive force is misdirected or abused are legendary. At the same time the benefits of its containment within the vows of marriage as well as the channeling of its primitive energies into higher expressions are equally noteworthy. In the scheme of evolution it is the intention of the Creator that this procreative force gradually makes its way up the spinal cord, entering each of the chakras within each of the higher bodies. When this kundalini fire advances far enough, lust, aggression, hate, prejudice and bondage cease. For example, while on the astral plane it generates emotional desire, on the mental plane it manifests as the thought form of parenthood underlying this aspect of man's or woman's destiny. Turning again to the chakras, the heart chakra responding to this sacred fire causes one to love deeply and universally. At the throat chakra it creates fearless, true and indelible words of life.

Only in recent years, particularly in the healing lines of inquiry, has research begun to fathom the nature of the chakras. Much about these sacred centers still remains veiled in mystery. On the causal plane, for instance, the chakras respond differently. They are more upturned and the two lower chakras begin to fade out of the picture, having served their usefulness. Regarding our inner bodies, in place of the physical spinal cord itself, a filament forms which conducts the life force or primal energy from God Supreme. At the same time, this transformation sets in motion the two other divine forces: vitality from the Solar Logos and the kundalini fire from the Planetary Logos. In their very highest regions these impulses stir to life the will to work for the fulfillment of new causes and the attainment of moral enlightenment and refined character. All the while, the upper range of chakras, as they come into their unfoldment, opens the door of inner perception and conscious out-of-body travel.

The spleen chakra lies in the lower left side of the abdomen in the organ from which its name derives. Its function is to receive vitality currents from the sun and distribute them throughout each individual's being. A medley of colors radiates through this center—red, orange, green, blue, yellow, and violet. This second chakra contains six spokes reflecting these colors. In a physically healthy person, the spleen chakra expands to a width of at least six inches. When a person is ill, it contracts noticeably in size and the colors lose their brightness, turning pale. Walks in the out-of-doors, working in gardens, and active visits to nature citadels all greatly benefit this chakra. Those who are its natural recipients have about them an aliveness and an abundance of energy—in a word, they possess vitality.

The navel chakra lies at that part of our anatomy so named: it is also known as our solar plexus chakra. It is the most sensitive of the seven chakras, detecting vibrations that are all about us. When things are not right according to its sensors, this chakra accelerates suddenly, causing its classic response, a disturbed or sinking sensation in the pit of the stomach. Its main function is to be our early warning system, informing us of what lies ahead: harmony or discord, order or chaos, safety or danger. Known psychologically as the sub-conscious brain, it is our survival sentry "waiting daily at our gates; watching at the posts of our doors." Since many, if not most, of our worries or fears are either groundless or greatly exaggerated, we need to carefully examine our concerns, weeding out the foolish ones. Only by striving for ever greater self-control, a sense of detachment from trivial happenings, and a deepening of our faith, will this center stabilize and experience peace. On the other hand, since we live in a world that can expose us to threatening circumstances and real dangers, we will need to cultivate a healthy vigilance when in fact we are at risk.

Interestingly, this center doesn't explain itself or give reasons why a particular concern or problem exists. It simply reflects its feelings at the moment. When reasons come they arrive from the higher chakras on the mental plane and provide good insight into the meaning and value of persons, creatures, circumstances, and things. For example, the heart chakra gives us insight into the particular feelings of compassion or spiritual love we might have for a given individual. On the other hand, it could warn us of the untrustworthiness or duplicity of another. It is the keeping of this keen edge of discernment that each soul must eventually master without being sentimentally naive toward those we like or blindly prejudiced against those we dislike. In other words, beyond our feelings lie the understandings as to why—this is what brings us to wisdom in our relationships.

This third chakra contains ten spokes; its colors are red and green. Worry darkens these colors by introducing a grey overcast, while faith and courage brighten them. It is also the chakra most readily accelerated by the God light from the Spirit Indwelling.

The heart chakra has its center at the heart's location in the chest and is the highest chakra that most persons have activated at this point of human evolution. The fifth, sixth and seventh chakras are mostly undeveloped in the population at large. Nevertheless, a significant number of individuals will be in beginning to advanced stages of awakened unfoldment, and such persons will not be neglected. Of all the centers, the heart chakra is usually the largest, reflecting the loving, compassionate and unselfish nature of the awakening soul. Exceptions to this trend are the purely mental types whose heart chakras are relatively small.

For this chakra a rose hue predominates, its twelve spokes radiating various intensities of blue. The higher the soul, the more this center radiates pink; however, advanced initiates occasionally possess golden radiations in place of the blue.

It is in the heart chakra that the God Spirit Indwelling has its residence. Its brilliant golden light shines out sometimes as if a gap existed in the auric robe formed by the higher bodies, allowing this much of its wondrous light to shine through. The heart chakra marks the beginning of the higher range of energy centers that prepares us for illumination. Its unfoldment comes with greater love and a more caring attitude expressed for each human being, creature, tree, flower and every form of life. Finally, the more unselfishly we love, the more will spiritual energies flow into the heart chakra through any or all of its twelve spokes.

This brings us to the throat chakra which has to do with our voice and how we make use of it. Its finest function is to put into words spiritual truth. Singers, speakers, teachers, executives, all people who use their voices in presenting, counseling, and communicating have expanded throat chakras.

When used constructively, this chakra empowers us to speak in a way that inspires others. What makes this difference is that our speaking has its source in God. We are then using the energy of the kundalini fire as it was intended. If, on the other hand, a person is negative in vocal expression, the chakra turns counterclockwise, making the individual excessively talkative or nervous in their manner of speech.

When we are with other people, it is wise to observe silence as much as engaging in conversation. One needs time to reflect and assimilate, as much as to give voice to one's thoughts and feelings. Unless you allow these spaces of silence, you run the danger of aimless chatter when what is far more satisfying and beneficial is a period of quiet reflection in which to love persons from deep within.

The color of the throat chakra is a bright leaf-green along with a medium blue, with soft white radiations emanating from some of the points of force. There are sixteen petal-like spokes.

Sixth in order is the brow chakra which is located in the forehead between and slightly above our two physical eyes. It has an opalescent sheen for a background with light blue and light green emanations alternating with those of a rose-violet hue. There are ninety-six spokes in this center. This forms what is known as the "third eye" that brings with it the gift of inner sight.

Not until clairvoyance begins to unfold does this chakra actually possess color and beauty, all of which brings us to an important caution. There is associated with inner sight a certain glamour, a fortune-telling atmosphere, a fascination with phenomena, that is both superficial and dangerous. It is superficial because it only deals with the surface of inner perception—that which catches the fancy of public curiosity.

It is dangerous because it quickly becomes driven by the ego once it finds an audience. To be safe and secure, inner perception is only trustworthy when it is guided by strong self-discipline, balanced by an emerging wisdom and a selfless motivation to help others.

There is another way to go, one that is relatively free of the drawbacks posed by a premature claim to clairvoyance, yet is still one of the precursors to authentic inner sight. This is intuition — the immediate grasp of truth that comes to us in the form of promptings, impressions, insights, and realizations discussed in Chapter Five. Moreover, intuition is far more universal and acceptable as a function than clairvoyance, which has a mixed history, much of which is not easily validated.

To earn good marks in either intuition or clairvoyance, one must *live the life*, a major prerequisite for coming of age spiritually. And the first condition that living the life asks of us is a coming to purification—freeing ourselves of all self-serving habits that stand in our way so we can make room for what lies ahead that is new and holds promise for the future of ourselves.

The activation of the brow chakra coincides with the onset of our own spiritual awakening. We are entering that phase of our individual evolution when we begin experiencing a series of major and minor initiations and their subsequent illuminations. Perception, which until this juncture has been preoccupied with outer reality, now encounters inner reality and our experience of life undergoes one transformation after another. There is a major shift in activity among the chakras, with the lower ones becoming less active and the higher ones more so. Of all the changes awaiting us in life, this awakening of inner perception is the most profound and light-filled. It is no less than the sunrise itself, for it unveils one revelation after another. Such is the great adventure of seeing ever more deeply into the heart of reality.

Finally we come to the crown chakra. Whereas the brow chakra serves as our sixth sense, the crown chakra expresses our seventh sense. Its unfoldment allows individuals to consciously step out of their physical bodies and travel into the inner worlds. Prior to this conscious ability, we have the use of this skill only at night when we journey to various locations for instruction. To protect us from becoming disconnected from our earthly body, an etheric cord of electric energy holds fast to our physical form, ensuring our safe return. With the full functioning of the crown chakra, this form of travel can now occur consciously and at the command of the awakened soul in the company of one's Guardian Angel. It is a wondrous ability to step out into the Inner Worlds, fully aware of the fact, visiting the Halls of Learning in Shamballa, the New Jerusalem, great citadels of light, or even other planets.

One other important function of this chakra is its role in our releasement at death. At its appointed time it sends a surge of electrical current throughout the physical and etheric bodies, ceasing their function. This leaves the astral body as the means for the graduating soul to return to the Inner Worlds and its homeland.

The crown chakra is most beautiful: 960 lines of force emanate from its hub. The colors of its flower-like petals range from violet to orchid, interspersed with yellow.

Taken in sequence, these seven chakras form a chain of evolutionary unfoldment. The first two centers—the root and spleen chakras—basically serve a physiological function and are vital to the health and well-being of our physical bodies. The navel and heart chakras respond particularly to our personal feelings and provide the fuel for our coming to self-conquest and maturity. The three highest chakras—the throat, brow, and crown—are governed by our awakening soul and are the gates through which flow the currents of illumination and initiation. In that order each center unfolds its channeling of divine energy.

In conclusion, one final word about the most mysterious of the forces flowing up the spinal cord. We have mentioned previously what in the east is called the kundalini fire. Seen clairvoyantly on every plane of its existence from the physical to the monad it indeed appears as a flame burning brightly. Its effects, when wisely directed, are wondrous. It generates the life force enabling a couple to reproduce and bring forth children. It is the source of the light, the beauty, and the vision that makes a gifted soul creative. It is the sunrise of enlightenment experienced by a mystic. And it is the purifying fires of mastery that illuminate an adept.

This sacred flame has its beginning within each person as he or she sets out on the extraordinary journey in the school of life. As the individual gradually makes progress, the kundalini fire makes its way up the spinal cord, igniting one chakra after another. As each center is activated, it marks a milestone in that individual's progress such that in the incarnation following that attainment, each of these achievements is briefly experienced anew, reestablishing its presence and reality. It is evolution's way of reminding us of our progress.

What is important to realize and appreciate about chakras is their responsiveness to our constructive attention. For example, we long for the will to live a more refined and en-lightened life, and if we exercise that will, all of these centers increase their clockwise motion. If we are inspired by the exampleship of a great soul, past or present, the brow and crown chakras in particular stir into action. If, during the holy week preceding Christmas or Easter, we sense the inner currents that accompany these potent spiritual periods, again the chakras are more receptive and open their gates wider than usual.

It is for us to remember that when we are out of tune or otherwise disconnected from these higher energies—when negatively preoccupied—we risk a breakdown of their normal state of well-being. Once any one of these centers weakens, by suffering abuse or neglect, we are opening the door to malfunctioning or to disease itself. In fact, all disturbed or abnormal states are accompanied by a reversal of motion in the chakras, causing them to turn counterclockwise in contrast to the usual clockwise direction. It is this condition that underlies the various symptoms of illness or distress telling us that all is not well within. Correcting this situation through prayer, visualization, and the willingness to change our outlook and expectancy are essential.

How much wiser for us to take this initiative and to focus on the attuned unfoldment of this vital energy system by recognizing its reality and by working toward its harmonious, healthful evolution.

We are entering a millennium that will recognize and celebrate the reality of these fascinating energy centers. The entire enterprise of holistic medicine is already involved in their activation and healthful functioning. It is time to realize the value of the chakras and by means of our skillful use of visualization to create a conscious connection in our meditation work with each one.

Chapter 9
Governing Our
Atomic Intelligences

We have nearly completed the review of our sevenfold nature. We have realized how these several vehicles ascend in their significance; the lower four forming the basic components with which we function in the physical world and the other three forming the upper triad which comes into play as we awaken to God and the Inner Worlds.

We have also examined the seven chakras whose energies play such an important role in our well-being.

What remains is an even more mysterious and extraordinary realm—that of the atomic intelligences. Each of the sevenfold bodies is composed of trillions of these tiny elementals which are sensitive to either our neglect or our focused attention. Given their vital role in our health and wholeness, it is essential that we cultivate the latter.

These infinitesimally minute specks of energy spin like stars in a miniature universe and are the building blocks of all that we are. What is so very important is to address these elemental generators of life from the level of our souls, visualizing and becoming aware of their reality. Awareness, in fact, is the threshold we cross in approaching the invisible. Let us bless these myriads of atomic intelligences with goodwill which radiates a deep faith in their power to uplift us and lay the foundation for our evolutionary progress.

By their very nature, the atoms composing the monad, adonai, and soul are free of disturbances or imbalances. We begin, therefore, with the mental body causing its atoms to face Godward and to feel the soul's purity pouring out its light upon the atomic formation that is the mind. We next send forth a commandment of love and hope for our mental faculties to function peacefully and responsively to Divinity's light. We need to intuitively survey these bodies to realize improved memory, increased knowledge, and accelerated intelligence.

In a like manner, let the light of spirit illuminate the atomic intelligences comprising our emotional or astral vehicles. It is these vehicles that are the most unruly and prove to be the most disobedient to spirit. With deepest love we next extend the light of spirit in prayer to the countless atomic presences comprising these vehicles, for they form the means by which most of us enter the Inner Worlds at night. With the same loving command used previously, order these vehicles to cease their childishness and their attraction to instinctive emotions. Redirect these emotions such that they long instead for the serenity that arises from all that is beautiful and ennobling.

We now focus the light of spirit upon the nebulous form of our etheric bodies. Of all seven of our vehicles, this one is the most easily disturbed and most responsive to influential forces, positive or negative. Feel the soul releasing currents of love upon the etheric body, all the while envisioning its constructive response. Clairvoyantly, one normally sees whirling electrical fields, light rose in color, whose lines of force point downward as they release energy. With concerted effort, we project a most concentrated beam of blessing upon the trillions of atomic intelligences composing the etheric vehicle. Being highly responsive, etheric atoms turn quickly to the presence of light. As these intelligences turn their currents upward and Godward, the effect is transforming. Once experienced, the prayer is imprinted with the responsiveness of the etheric vehicles which is accompanied by a distinct sense of body lightness. We wisely intone the *blue spirit of prana* to bring new life into being for it is this prana that restores the etheric atoms, endowing them with unfailing vitality.

The sensitivity of these etheric atoms to a sudden change of tempo or mood greatly impacts them. Should we shift abruptly from a mood of joyousness and veneration to one of impatience and aggressiveness, this state causes these atoms to cease radiating energy in an outgoing manner and turns their whirls of power downward. Unfortunately this is not a position in which they can be revitalized. It requires the upward arc of their circulating energies to be consciously attained. Once that is reestablished through the strong focusing of prayer and visualization, a normal flow of etheric energy returns.

Likewise, direct God light from the Spirit Indwelling through the command and attention of the soul, into the physical body. Of utmost importance when dealing with this physical dimension is the third chakra, the subconscious brain, for it is the chakra most receptive to beneficial acceleration. As the forces comprising our vitality flow either downward or upward throughout the whole physical organism, it is this center that controls the outcome and is most receptive to our intervention. We must learn to speak lovingly and with firmness to our subconscious brain in such a way that wins its instantaneous obedience.

Now, with the same loving firmness, and beginning with the head region, visualize the countless myriads of atoms that constitute the region of our heads, both its bone structure and inner matter. Speak to the intelligences forming this vital component of our physical form by name, especially if any particular element needs attention.

Move the light to the throat region, focusing it there. As with the head, speak to the intelligences serving the throat and all of its structures. If there is a thyroid abnormality, ask it to return to its archetypal pattern of functioning and vitality as the Supreme Creator intended.

Then moving slowly throughout the entire body, direct your attention to all that remains, including the right and left sides of the body separately. In each instance address the particular organ or physical component by name and ask that it follow the form and function intended by God. Center a great deal of attention upon those parts or organs that are faulty. Urge the subconscious brain throughout all the hours and years of your life to give watchful support to that region. To the organ or member itself, the message can vary each day, but its substance must include the divine command to respond constructively and completely to the archetype of perfect functioning according to its purpose.

As you remember these wondrously conceived atomic intelligences that comprise our being, call upon them to vibrate agelessness. They hold the possibility to be endowed through their own receptivity with solar energies motivating them from deep within.

In coming to a command of these countless atomic intelligences, it is essential to know the specialized nature of three electrical rings that circle each atom. Only when these bands of force are functioning rhythmically together and at the same rate of speed will the intelligence locked within each of these rings stir and influence its whole miniature world.

The innermost band of force composing each atom is called the *edam ring*. It contains the memory of nature storing all of the impressions that have accumulated across the many lifetimes each individual has experienced. To be released from the backlog of negative impressions that inevitably have amassed across the centuries, it is necessary, working diligently, to keep the edam ring within each atom active in accumulating constructive impressions. This endeavor in time feeds the whole atom with joyous and positive energies. The time will come when the strength of these wholesome forces deliberately chosen by man's conscious decisions will purify and transform all of the latent negatives into new accumulations of constructive powers. When this has been achieved, the individual will no longer be influenced by any force of the past or recurrence of its memories.

The middle band of force is called the *poreas ring* and requires our utmost care and attention. Should this ring become disturbed and its rhythm broken due to improper thinking, feeling, or living, it may move counterclockwise and its pattern may become feeble. Moreover, when treated carelessly it becomes the means by which entire atoms and their radiating centers begin to decay or degenerate, inviting disease and the gradual cessation of life.

The poreas ring contains the design for the shape of our physical bodies. In fact, it is constantly discharging energies which impregnate the hereditary genes of this vehicle. When these genes are very active, the physical inheritances from such an individual will be strong and definite. This band of energy is continually influencing that which each one of us will further unfold in relation to the stored inheritance factors constituting our family tree.

Parents who fail to impress their children with any of their likenesses lack genes of vigor. The cause for this is a poorly rotating and weakened poreas ring. If this band of force can be cleansed from all friction, all poor functioning and weakened effort and then impressed with positive recordings attuning such an individual to forces of health, then it is quite possible that ill health and other inherited afflictions will not be handed down after all.

The third and outermost band of force is called the *orium ring* and its mission is life-giving. This is the radiant energy source revolving around every atom's world. Like a physical sun, it moves at immense speeds and as it moves it gives life. It broadcasts and radiates the forces released by the atom throughout the whole of the entire vehicle in which it is active. We know the electrical radiation it yields as cosmic rays.

Should, for example, atoms in the physical foot be injured, it affects all three rings. It is the third ring, however, that would be noticeably handicapped by the slower rhythm of this ring and its inability to discharge electrical energies into the field of its radiating center.

The orium ring is unusual in that its mission is to bring up from the center of the atom electrical chargings that it broadcasts, giving life to the body. Depending on the strength of its discharges an individual will experience radiant or weakened health. This ring is the most sensitive and influential of the three energy bands along with being the widest in its radiating qualities. This makes it especially receptive to conscious influence. If our outlook is optimistic and keenly supportive, the orium ring comes into harmony with this positive expectancy and the door is open for an upsurge in our energy level. If, on the other hand, we are unconvinced of the method itself or if we are just going through the motions, the response will be indefinite and lacking in strength. The orium rings are particularly responsive to pleasing us when we are faith-filled and eager and address them with a commanding reverence that invites new unfoldments. It is the orium ring that holds the key to returning to health sick or aging organs, or transforming a downcast or rebellious spirit.

The rims of the atoms contain the forces which form the treasures that each person has accumulated. When an individual completes his or her experience of life, all of the atomic energies that have been gathered in this one's life comprising that treasure are stored in the akashic records.

Therein lies the disciple's work — to learn how to command the atomic intelligences to work in rhythm, each band resplendently encircling the atom on fire with its beneficent qualities, releasing highly tuned electrical energies into each person's entire aura.

As a further treatment, following your regular meditation and prayer efforts, invite and welcome the flow of God's light into each of your sevenfold vehicles beginning with the God-flame. After a moment's reflection visualizing this infusion of Divinity's sunrise in your God Self, see the passage of this light flowing on into your adonai, pronouncing it by name and recognizing it as the body which channels and holds the God light. Next, see the light entering the soul and then, in order, the other four vehicles, briefly cleansing, renewing and strengthening all of the trillions of atoms that each vehicle contains. As you proceed in this treatment, direct the atoms into new patterns of unfoldment before addressing the rings themselves. Then turn your attention to these vital energy bands, speaking the word for clearing of all three rings in all of your bodies at one time.

On another occasion, to deepen your work with the atoms and your assuming their command, at the conclusion of the treatment of the three rings, say: "And let the flow of Infinite God light enter the heart of the atom, making it a glowing center — a veritable sun. Let my body, on every plane of expression, be composed of light which proceeds from innumerable suns within me."

In conclusion, the recognition of this miniature universe within each one of us that forms the building blocks of which all seven of our bodies are composed, gives to our meditation work an extraordinary opportunity. Mastership itself consists of pure and attained conquest of every atomic body with which one has to deal. In working with the atomic intelligences, the Master inspiring these revelations made a profound statement: *"He who is able to govern the atoms of any particular region is able to govern life."*

Chapter 10
The Four Elements

In reviewing the many files of lectures and writings by Flower A. Newhouse to obtain material on the seven bodies, a relationship between these and the four kingdoms of nature came to light. As the latter contained information of value in illuminating how the seven bodies themselves function, this chapter presents highlights of her teachings about each of the four kingdoms as they relate to the understanding of ourselves.

One other point in dealing with the four elements: it is well to know that the fire kingdom is joined symbolically to the cardinal point east; the air kingdom to the west; and the water kingdom to the south and the earth kingdom to the north. Therefore, whenever it is expedient to align ourselves for deepening associations with these kingdoms, endeavor to face in their respective directions.

Fire

Fire is considered to be the most pure and the most Godly element. Our lives originated in the divine fiery substance of the One called God. Our spirit which is a portion of the Godhead is a pure flame composed of form and properties that are wondrously mysterious and beyond the grasp of our understanding. Another interesting observation — in its source the flame of life is without heat because of the absence of friction. Eventually, as conditions creating friction are encountered, heat is generated.

This flame, at one with the pure element of the fiery life of God the Whole, projects its powers into the planet until physical existence is made possible. Wherever these life currents flow, properties related to fire will be found, which include electricity, heat, light and movement.

Without the intention of the Godhead in each of us to experience the objectivity of physical life as the earth offers it, we could not find or build residences here. Think of the ways in which the life stream circulates throughout our bodies. Our blood carries the element of heat and through its temperature we know the fire of life. Our heart, under the will of spirit, furnishes movement which constitutes life as we know it in a physical body. In our astral vehicle, the fire of the spirit is expressed as ardor, enthusiasm, incentive, the will for progress, and the determination for conquest.

Notice that nothing has been said of human desire, for in every way the fire of life is pure and one-pointed. When we meditate concerning the health of our bodies, it is with the recognition that the spirit's intention is for a purified life.

In our astral or emotional vehicle, whenever we come near to actual and genuine whole-heartedness, we are in tune with the flame of our spirit.

On the mental plane, our life current expresses itself expansively as the energizing of the enterprise of knowledge. Again the flame's vitality is carried into this realm and pupils come alive intellectually when their interests and their thoughts are one-pointedly open and receptive; when they are searching and scanning the horizons of daily encounters for the intuitive impulses that will empower them to further mental progress.

On the soul plane the currents carrying the life force are known for their spontaneity, wholesome naturalness, and innate beauty. Their predominant mode of expression always is through intuitions which arrive out of the blue, fully formed, and with surprising simplicity.

In the adonaic realm the life force becomes more dominant and wholly focused on the essence of purity. There are no alloys here, no mixtures, no conflicts to disturb the serenity of the flame of vibrant life consciousness beating energetically in tune with the rhythm of creation.

In summary, to realize a life that is healthy, joyous and triumphant, it is necessary to come into a condition of purity — purity of intentions and motivations. We humans are inclined to compromise the truth in order to fashion false impressions, gain favor, avoid criticism or unpleasant encounters, all of which come home to haunt us.

To realize movement toward this condition of purity, we would do well to choose a day in which to give our creative attention to achieving a genuineness of motivation. Hereafter, whenever we aspire to improve or perfect our health, let us consider first reestablishing a one-pointed alignment with integrity; we should never compromise with the genuineness of the flame within us. We should never seek to veil the light by giving consideration to others that would make us untrue to the same flame within. Moreover, we need to remember it is essential to keep ourselves free from the mixtures of conflicting interests, however noble. We need to realize the value of sincerity and purity of intention and its uplift to our outlook. We need to consider the blessedness of wisely keeping the body unalloyed from the poisons which the instinctive nature would invite. It is important to strengthen our emotional natures such that they can purely and strongly express enthusiasm. We want to recall each day the will and the ardor that must come from the spirit within to prepare for understanding and mastering the details of a continuously growing mentality.

It is then for us to find the simplicity the soul knows in pursuing its vital purposes, paying heed to its intuitional instructions. Then during at least one of our remembrance times we would be wise to practice recollection upon the fire of life and the electrical chargings flowing through our spirit within. To have its wave-lengths realized unbrokenly through to the physical body itself there must be excellent rapport built up between all the vehicles of consciousness. Daily we need to remember to invite life experiences that are as pure as the God-flame within each of us—a flame that is all-consuming of the unreal. We then can allow it to enter and be fully active within our consciousness such that we know the peace of God that surpasses understanding.

Air

The air kingdom originates within the great ensouling wisdom of Deity. Of the four kingdoms, air is most closely associated with consciousness. On the mental plane it manifests as mentality. On the soul plane it forms the wings of direct perception through the faculty of intuition. On the adonaic level it becomes the throne of all-knowing wisdom. Wherever there is wisdom one finds movement, birth and generation of the new. Indeed, presiding over the entire air kingdom are those extraordinary beings in charge of the Third Aspect of the Holy Trinity—those who determine the pathways of growth leading to enlightenment.

In our own vehicles, the lungs are the symbolic receptors of this kingdom's benefits. Into our lungs pour not only the ingredients which oxidize, purify and accelerate our physical vehicles, but which simultaneously inbreathe into our higher bodies the movements of divine wisdom, divine will, and divine causation.

The air kingdom makes one demand, that humans realize thanksgiving for the gift of wisdom as well as for the continuation of individual existence. Henceforth, we need to recall frequently with every intake of breath that we are inbreathing God's wisdom, God's permeation, and God's quickening into every center of our existence. We must become conscious with each physical breath we take that we are breathing astrally, mentally, causally, adonaically, and divinely, all at the same time.

It is requisite that we consider air as a very sacred instrument since it carries frequencies to us, not only from the highest initiate who is visible to us in the Solar Logos, but in addition it brings surges of wavelengths from the regions of Godhood.

Whenever we breathe it is helpful to recall that we are breathing the thoughts of God and they are setting into action the stimulus which will free or generate new states that either we need when they are positive or must have no part of when they are negative. There is something about advanced souls at times that amounts to the fragrance of sanctity. When this condition is present it indicates a kinship on their part to the lofty frequencies from the causal world. Whenever we breathe a cleansing breath, which must be a very deep and penetrating one, we inwardly align ourselves to the spirit of God which is in us.

The spirit is not only flame-like but its movements beget activations of currents whose energies we know as the vibrations that produce sound. When once we cultivate a clean body and we have earned, through nobler living, a clean breath and a constant remembrance of tuning in to the presence of spirit with each breath, then we are ready for the gifts of spirit, particularly of extrasensory hearing.

The beings in charge of the air kingdom, as it originated within the Spirit of God and until it descends to the surface of earth, are most difficult for man to contact. The lordly and intensely impersonal fire devas are more inclined to respond to appeal than the citizenry of the air world. This is because their very beings require uninterrupted alignment with resources of energy that they take in with each breath consciously drawn. Their nearness at times to the earth's aura brings them their principal testings. When such a descent is necessary for these pure, lighted ones, it is like dipping momentarily into the gases of a most obnoxious substance. For that reason we do not find many of the lordly ones of the air in the vicinity of cities. They are always present where the altitude is high and the prana emanating from the vastness of the region is very noticeable.

Should we need or desire access to such beings we may have communion with them on the condition that we first prepare ourselves by the inward cleansing of our bodies, breath, along with our thoughts and radiations. Our thoughts are the air currents moving into and playing through us, from the mental world. At those times when we are conscious of the enjoyment of deep breathing, we need to recall these beings, the hosts of them, and the octaves of their gradations that attend to the sounding of God's word: without the medium of air there can be no sound.

That great and tremendous chorus creating the music of the spheres, is composed mainly of inhabitants of the air kingdom. Seldom will one find earth, water or fire citizens among this body.

Water

All the debris in the emotional nature which consists of struggles, frustrations, depressions and impurities, is expelled through this flow of superior healing waters. We need to persist in inviting and permitting this flow through from the loftiest levels of consciousness until we are aware that every particle of this moment's bitterness, unhappiness or impurity is being cleansed. Time and again the barriers of our instinctive natures will build their dams which we consciously must destroy through the reception to the strong currents of the wholesome, wondrous, magical elements entering us from the higher recesses of our selfhood.

Water is used for baptism because it is so highly magnetic. Our emotions are likewise magnetic; in fact the astral body in its response to the flow of Eternal Will can be defined as radiations of magnetism through this faculty of consciousness.

Whenever we approach God the Most High in one-pointed, consecrated reverence, we are baptized anew with the everlasting waters flowing out of the Eternal Presence. It remains our obligation to transmute our entire water nature on every level of life, to broadcasting water blessings in the form of constructive emotions of the noblest order. We must see to it that our emotional natures and their outflow of personal magnetism are not of the kind which allow the winds of the instinctive nature to be aroused. We must allow our personal magnetism to be like the dew of heaven, wielding an influence which is itself fluidic, but in the manner of a strong river which creates new canyons while it moves along its patient way.

In the Bible, wine has always held a significant place because it referred not to fermented drinks but to the wholesome properties of fruit mingled with water. The wine of life within each of us is found in our soulic and adonaic natures. Here is strength, untrammeled joy, and praise unceasing. In our times of inward communion we will remember that the flow of life as it reaches us through the water world brings us the unfermented wine or the fruit and water cleansings from the highest sources.

When we need the waters of our feelings cleansed more deliberately, we must ask for the spiritual wine of life to be brought to us that we may be fed on the interior plane of being.

Whenever we deal with water as in bathing, drinking, swimming, or observing, remember here is a most sensitive element whose citizenry requires from man his conquest of destructive emotions. As you drink water, hold aloft your glass prayerfully saying, "May this water, sensitively subjected as it always is to the intake of spiritual and alchemical influences, release through me as it enters me, all stains, all impurities and all clinging things of my conscious as well as my unconscious habits." Whenever we look upon water or partake of it, we need to realize that through its vital charging, its highly magnetic cleansing properties, we too may know releasement, refreshment, purification, and especially delight.

Earth

We have seen that the fire element has its origin in the very spirit of God and our spirit receives its light from the Infinite God-fire. We have learned that the air kingdom has a relationship to the Divine Wisdom of our own spirit and the water kingdom has its highest attribute within the spiritual will which resides within us.

We will consider finally the earth and the part it plays in radiating the life element completely through every vehicle to the very physical vestment itself.

Life, when resident in the physical body, has found its most grim imprisonment when compared to the freedom that exists for all the other bodies and their corresponding planes comprising the Inner Worlds. Perhaps the most grossly enclosed vehicle of life that can be found lies within the rocks and the minerals of earth. A little freer expression of this life grows within the plant world. A further releasement is active in the animal kingdom. The more joyous and more liberated form of this life pressing out into manifestation is evident in man. Life which is truly released and triumphant is to be noted in the lives of the perfected souls who comprise the ranks of earth's graduates.

The element earth is restrictive in its purpose and this is intentional. There needs to be confinement in order that specific disciplines can be evolved by means of these restrictions. Our physical forms are not only the most dense but likewise they are the smallest of our seven vehicles. With every act of regeneration we achieve, we are causing our bodies to come that much closer to eternity—in the words of the initiate Paul, to put on *immortality*. It is through the restrictions imposed by physical reality that each aspirant comes to the conquest of self-government and the mastery of the disciplines which form the path Godward.

There are two turns in the road of physical life. One leads into the manifest physical body and the other comes into existence on the plane invisible to physical sight but still etherically a part of the earth world.

Those of us who have taken on the forms of solid matter for countless lives are closely related to those who have taken the etheric branch of unfoldment and who are evolving equally in their etheric vehicles. These numerous beings who form the earth kingdom of the nature world have sizes that vary from that comparable to the tiniest insect to a figure equal to the size of tall hills.

These are the citizenry with which we should become more affiliated. Their demand in accepting the companioning of human beings is one primarily of unselfishness.

Until man comes to the regenerate life, his associations with this etheric realm are not trustworthy. As a result, and in defense of their world, these etheric beings do what they can to counteract man's carelessness and ambition by utilizing trickery. They practice deceits, not with the purpose of inflicting harm, but because of man's selfishness, they mislead him, drawing him away from the discovery of the jewels, treasures and other benefits of earth. When the time comes that man realizes the importance of being in harmony with nature, the entire relationship changes. Then he finally comes to the deep appreciation of these etheric citizens. The more he adventures along the path of his own conquest, the better and more bountifully will their guidance and favors rest with him.

The body has frequently been called foursquare by the very nature of its solidarity. It has both positive and negative circumstances with which one must deal intelligently. The body is circumscribed and limited, yet if wisely directed from within, can become the firm foundation upon which masterhood can build. Since we are still in physical form with many lives ahead of us, we need to deal with our bodies in a manner by which their very limitations are turned toward the good. Being of small stature relatively speaking, we cannot know the strength, power, ability, nor the liberation of the air citizenry. Their bodies are tenuous and so much more elastic, moving rhythmically according to their slightest indications. By contrast, our inability to conquer space on our own motive power such as by flying or expanding ourselves physically into giants, is simply a condition we must bear. We benefit most by confining our territory of interest, challenge and attainment to our present circumstances. For that reason, the more circumspect we become in this incarnation and the more one-pointed, the faster will be our transcendence and our mastery of physical incarnation.

Above all things, earth citizens have to learn the lesson of patience. Their very confinements are irksome becoming detriments to our inner conquests. We must permit our four-square natures to rest easily upon their solid foundation of mother earth. Our need is to be faithful, practical, reliable, unselfish and persistent in our human forms while yet we wear these bodies. We have other capacities for flight, for the reception of creativity, or the enlargements of consciousness. These can only express themselves when the physical body upon which they depend is truly and securely well-controlled.

Our object lessons during the times of our more advanced unfoldment point directly toward our achievements of conscious control—the putting on of immortality through the regeneration and enlightenment of our interests and desires. Each day, those who stand at our place of unfoldment need to remind ourselves, "I must prove that I who use this body am not its slave but its director. I choose the way of immortalizing my physical body by adopting and cultivating the habits and decisions of refinement and of spiritual transformation."

We need to treat our bodies wisely. Be kind to them. Respect them, for ours is an ageless work in their regard. Most of the atoms of our present physical vehicles, when we are finished with them, will become the vestment of those who have reached the place in growth where now we stand. And, if we merit or earn the right, those beyond us shall endow us with their atomic robes so that we may temporarily wear them in our turn on this plane of matter and force, called earth.

Every sunrise should find us meditating upon the manner by which we may improve the realm of our consciousness leading to illumination and the purification of our emotional nature. Also, in as many details as we can master, we must tirelessly pursue the care and well-being of our physical bodies as a worthy and valued investment in our future incarnations and as a gift in gratitude to our Creator.

Conclusion

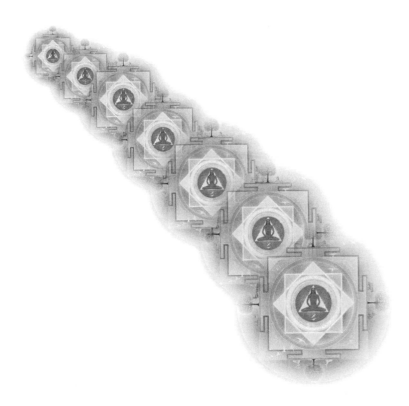

The preceding chapters have shared a wealth of knowledge about the seven bodies, the seven chakras, the atomic intelligences, and the four elements of nature. This knowledge, however, means little unless it is put into practice. It is the aim of this final chapter to address this need and propose ways of utilizing this wisdom in the service of the light.

A great barrier to knowing is the nature of things invisible. We humans are so dependent on what our five senses tell us that energies that lie beyond the visible spectrum or the audible range tend to be ignored. Even though we believe in the existence of such phenomena, if we cannot readily see them, especially with the intent to observe their progress and transformation, we are inclined to pay them little heed. So it is that our first action must be fine-tuning our awareness to connect with these superphysical realities.

While we may not experience visible contact with these energy fields, one thing we can do is to intuitively feel their presence and their state of being. We know when we are depleted physically or when we possess an abundant energy reserve. The same is true emotionally or mentally. Our state of being is sensitive to the ups and downs that characterize these inner attributes. We know when we are at peace or otherwise preoccupied or troubled. We know when our minds are functioning smoothly or when they are scattered and error prone. We know when we are centered in the light of God's mantling or when we are out of accord with Divinity. In all three instances it is an inner sensing of well-being, or that of flatness or a disturbed state.

Fine-tuning our awareness by attending to the health of each of our bodies becomes an exercise we need to practice regularly. We know that from time to time one or more of our lower bodies will be tested. Each of these occasions can be noted in our journals, so that we have a record of what might have caused the disturbance along with what took place to bring it back to balance. It might be a physical challenge, lack of energy, an emotional upset, or a mental conflict. During these trials what matters is our response, and to benefit the afflicted body, our response needs to be both constructive and focused.

On the constructive side, the essential ingredient is a positive attitude. Where the seven bodies are concerned, always the expectation must be for better functioning. The best we can do is to create in consciousness the healthiest and most receptive state of mind of which we are capable.

Such an attitude goes beyond being positive—it is actually *envisioning it into life*, which brings it into focus. We picture the well-being of each body in as much detail as we are able. Granted, this is most readily done for the four lower bodies as they are more accessible, though each of the upper triad of bodies needs to be recognized and to the extent possible, experienced.

What we are dealing with that involves our attitude and its focus is consciousness. Of all the attributes that distinguish humans as endowed with a divine gift, consciousness is the most noteworthy. In the history of psychology it has proven to be at once the most elusive and yet the most obvious capacity that sets us apart from all other creatures on the planet. It is the means by which we accumulate knowledge and information, make decisions, solve problems, recall the past, anticipate the future, intuit the new and creative, and, most illuminating of all, experience enlightenment. Still, all of this is subject to our attitude—our point of view. If our attitude is fearful and pessimistic, we are inclined toward a dark view of life. If on the other hand it is positive and optimistic, we are inclined toward a light-filled forecast of what life holds for us. So significant is this simple fact that if we change how we see life, we change who we are.

The archetypal example of this phenomenon is Saul on the road to Damascus who encounters a vision of the Lord Christ, and in that instant is transformed into the Apostle Paul. Our own transformations are not likely to be that dramatic, but certainly they will change who we are.

What does all of this have to do with the preceding chapters? The answer is, *everything!* In a very real sense we create consciousness both by what we attend to and how we attend to it. Of the thousand and one things we could focus upon at any given moment, the one thing we select becomes who we are in that same moment. But it goes deeper. Not just the thing itself but how we regard it, is the essential question.

This viewpoint that reflects our regard is a matter of choice, and choice is a function of will. True, our regard often becomes so habitual that it comes on automatically without any deliberation or question. What constitutes our regard is who we are and the way life is at that moment. When we awaken to the realization of the Inner Worlds and our inner bodies, a series of transformations is set into motion such that our regard now becomes an act of will. We are free to bask in the comfort of self-satisfaction, if life is so accommodating, or rise above our lethargy and climb the Mountain of God.

Choice and will, then, are the means by which we marshal the discipline to take charge of our lives and set out on the Great Journey. Our commitment in this undertaking is to let our higher natures rule and lead. Having said this, it is essential to realize that such a declaration inevitably arouses a reaction that has been mentioned previously: confrontation with the human shadow—the instinctive nature that puts our wills to the test. It begins a war between our higher and lower natures that will last for the remainder of our incarnations, but it is a war that the soul within us is destined to win, though there may be battles lost before the final victory is gained.

In the conduct of this war, three of the most effective strategies the shadow relies on are discouragement, projection and neglect. Discouragement risks giving up the quest as beyond our capability. Projection places the responsibility for problems we encounter on other people or our unfortunate circumstances, holding ourselves blameless. Neglect, however, is a more cunning and debilitating mechanism because, without its making a fuss, we simply forget our good intentions. As a result, we avoid an overt confrontation with the shadow, yet at the same time, we gain no ground to benefit our soul.

The soul, on the other hand, has its own resources from which to draw. Among its most potent tools is centeredness in God, most consistently experienced when in meditation. It provides us with a direct connection to the soul and its intuitive wisdom. There is no more effective pathway to the exercise of choice and the activation of will than this.

Every moment we dwell in soulic consciousness brings us a moment closer to the transformation of how we see, how we experience life, how we appreciate the mystery of the Inner Worlds that comes with awakening to its illuminating reality. There is no finer example of this principle at work then the one who is the source of the preceding chapters, Flower A. Newhouse. It was in this manner that she came upon her favorite invocation. Of this discovery she writes,

"One morning in meditation I found myself guided along a new and untried path which led to the strongest and most intimate realization of the God Spirit Indwelling that I have ever encountered. It proved to be a technique of alignment with the indwelling adonai. Since this finding was made, contact with that inner Divine Spirit has unfolded a comprehension of God's immediate presence that has blessed many who have used it with spiritual peace and in ever-increasing measure." Here is the invocation she called the *alignment technique*:

My physical body, with its invisible etheric sheath, is the servant of Lord God Indwelling. (Pause and envision this linkage.)

My physical and etheric bodies are aligned with my astral body, the disciple of Lord God Indwelling. (Pause and envision.)

My astral body is aligned with my mental body, the pupil of Lord God Indwelling. (Pause and envision.)

My mental body is aligned with my soul, my angel self, obedient to Lord God Indwelling. (Pause and envision.)

My soul is aligned to my adonai, the center of my spiritual will, and at one with Lord God Indwelling. (Pause and envision.)

My adonai is aligned to my monad, the God-flame that is Lord God Indwelling. (Pause and envision.)

Flower later learned that the source of this invocation was a teaching Master working under the Lord Maha Chohan, the Holy Spirit. Hardly a day passed thereafter but what she opened her meditations with this declaration. Besides its value as a means of aligning the seven bodies, an obvious use of this invocation is as a framework for an in-depth meditation that addresses each of the bodies in detail, expanding on the key attributes of each.

Its end result is the awakening of intuition and the sixth sense. Their function, in contrast to logic and rational analysis, is to be receptive to insights, promptings and revelations that originate in the Inner Worlds and which we have the good fortune to receive. This brings us to the threshold dividing the traditional five senses from the emerging awareness of the Inner Worlds. It is the latter that opens the gates to inner perception — to see with the inward eye what lies behind the veil of the physical. It is in this realm that six of the seven bodies lie, invisible, and for all practical purposes, nonexistent, unless an intuitive link is established that bridges this separation. Because intuition, unlike logic, is not subject to our command but comes to us as a gift, we need to develop other means of its awakening.

A good beginning comes through awareness and visualization. Awareness is the act of becoming conscious, in this case of the Inner Worlds and all that those realms contain. To build such an awareness, we need to develop the technique of visualization, the art of picturing in our mind's eye scenes of the Inner Worlds. This needs to be more than an exercise in imagination, which is not bound to any inner reality. It needs to be our *receptivity* to the reality that is actually there. For the purposes of this volume, it is the human aura that we are dealing with which includes the seven bodies and the seven chakras. At the conclusion of every meditation, we need to ask to be made receptive to our aura. It is important to be patient and not be under any pressure. It is also important not to have any fixed expectations. The response might be visual but it could come as an intuition, which is equally valid. Flower taught that the awakening of the sixth sense can come either visually, in a form of clairvoyance, or intuitively in the form of an impression or realization. We need to ask to be mantled so that we will receive the authentic awareness or vision that awaits our contact.

In this connection it is most helpful to keep a journal. It records our progress—in particular, our highs and lows and what is associated with each of these. It becomes the log of our spiritual journey such that from its entries we begin to tell a story, and as this story unfolds we become engaged in its telling. Once this takes place we realize two things. First is that to a significant extent we can influence the outcome of the story by exercising choice and the will behind our choices. Second, despite our influences, much of the story, good or otherwise, happens, like it or not. This occurs for reasons of karmic obligations falling due, as well as good fortune we have earned. The one makes for a sense of control over our destiny, which is reassuring; the other makes for the experience of adventure full of challenges, surprises, and the inevitable twists and turns that characterize life.

A journal becomes your source of feedback indicating growth and change, as well as the seasons of spiritual drought when such transformations are absent altogether. We now have a basis for detecting patterns or events that are either helpful or troublesome in search for what works. Suppose in Chapter Two the discussion on prana catches our attention. We then follow a plan of exposure to prana over a period of time and record in our journal any changes in our energy levels or inner experiences during this period.

Another opportunity for self-assessment occurs in Chapter Four which suggests ways to exercise and energize the mind. A careful record of our explorations here could reveal new pathways for activating our mental faculties, including the elements of intelligence.

Indeed, when encountering problems or solutions involving any aspect of the journey Godward, we should wisely write them down. While the scope of this volume seems limited to a relatively narrow range of phenomena associated with the seven bodies, the reader will quickly discover that it connects with all other facets that comprise our spiritual wholeness. A journal captures this fact and opens the door to insights and revelations that no other mechanism affords.

One other value of a journal is as a reminder that the story it tells is ongoing and never-ending and needs to be recorded and kept alive. Like a ship's log, it is the verification of our many ports of call and our adventures upon the seven seas of life. More to the point, it is tracing the outlines of regions of the Inner Worlds we have touched and how these encounters have been life changing. Like mariners of old, we are just now venturing beyond the sight of familiar landmarks into the great unknown. Some among us have made the journey of discovery and returned to reveal to the rest of us the wonders that await our own finding. If we keep the faith, our journals will add to the growing body of wisdom that is the true destiny of space exploration in the third millennium — the space within us that only the awakening of the sixth sense can illumine.

Your Notes

Your Notes

Your Notes